Whole Body Reset Diet Cookbook

365 Days of Healthy and Delicious Recipes to Boost Metabolism, Get a Flat Belly and Live Healthier Your Midlife And Beyond

Mitchell McCarthy

Table of Contents

Introduction

An international board of doctors, nutritionists, and fitness experts approved The Whole Body Reset after it had been examined by a panel of more than one hundred of the organization's professional staff. The Whole Body Reset was developed by a nonprofit, nonpartisan organization for people over fifty. It also contains ground-breaking new research on the benefits of "protein timing" for people in their 40s and 50s. This study challenges current government advice, refutes the notion of sluggish metabolisms and "inevitable" weight gain, and transforms how people in their forties and fifties view food. The Whole Body Reset investigates how aging affects our bodies and how changing our diets to account for these changes may cause us to respond to exercise as if we were 20 to 30 years younger.

Breakfast and Smoothie Recipes

Mushroom-Bell Pepper Omelet

Preparation time: 15 minutes
Cooking time: 25 minutes
Serves: 4

Ingredients:
- 30 tsp garbanzo bean flour (chickpea flour)
- 2 cups water
- Sea salt, to taste
- freshly ground black pepper, to taste
- ½ cup unsweetened almond milk
- ½ of an onion, chopped
- ¼ cup fresh mushrooms, cut into slices
- ¼ cup red bell pepper, seeded and diced
- 1 tbsp chives, minced

Directions:

1. Set your oven to 350°F. Grease a pie pan very lightly.
2. In a bowl, add the flour, water, salt, pepper, and almond milk. Beat until thoroughly blended.
3. In another bowl, combine the mushrooms, bell pepper, and onion. Evenly distribute the veggie mixture on top. Evenly sprinkle with chives. For 20 to 25 minutes, bake.

4. Slice into equal-sized wedges with a knife, then serve.

Nutritional Information: Calories 149; Fat 2.33g; Sodium 134mg; Carbs 26.23g; Fiber 4.5g; Sugar 8.4g; Protein 7g

Scrambled Tofu and Veggies

Preparation time: 15 minutes
Cooking time: 15 minutes
Serves: 2

Ingredients:

- ½ tbsp olive oil
- 1 small onion, chopped finely
- 1 small red bell pepper, chopped finely
- 1 cup cherry tomatoes, chopped finely
- 1½ cups firm tofu, crumbled and chopped
- Pinch of cayenne pepper
- Pinch of ground turmeric
- Sea salt, to taste

Directions:

1. Set a skillet on the stovetop and adjust the heat to medium. First, warm up the oil.
2. After that, sauté the bell pepper and onion for about 4 minutes.
3. Add the cherry tomatoes, chopped, to the skillet. After that, cook for 1-2 minutes.

4. Cook the tofu for 6 to 8 minutes after adding the spices (turmeric, cayenne, and salt).
5. The present is hot.

Nutritional Information: Calories 378; Fat 20.3g; Sodium 147mg; Carbs 25.4g; Fiber 7.4g; Sugar 12.4g; Protein 31.7g

Blueberry Cake

Preparation time: 18 minutes
Cooking time: 7 hours
Serves: 6

Ingredients:

- 1 tbsp grape seed oil
- ¾ cup spelt flour
- ¾ cup teff flour
- ¼ tsp sea salt
- 1 cup coconut milk
- ⅓ cup agave
- ½ cup fresh blueberries

Directions:

1. Line a cake pan with parchment paper and grease with grapeseed oil. Place aside. Inspect the Instant Pot to make sure the cake pan will fit. Combine the teff flour and spelt flour in a bowl.

2. Add the salt and whisk everything together. Milk and agave should be combined in a different bowl. When the dry components are thoroughly incorporated or lumps start to form, stir the wet ingredients into the dry ingredients. Blueberries should be added last.

3. Fill the cake pan with the combined batter after greasing it. Close the cover after adding the ingredients to the Instant Pot. Verify that the vent's setting is not "sealing." Set the cooking period at seven hours.

Nutritional Information: Calories 289; Fat 13g; Sodium 109mg; Carbs 38.8g; Fiber 6.2g; Sugar 4.8g; Protein 7.5g

Gingered Zucchini Bacon

Preparation time: 8 minutes plus 5 hours for marinating
Cooking time: 6 minutes
Serves: 4

Ingredients:

- 3 zucchinis, sliced thinly lengthwise or into large strips
- ¼ cup date sugar
- ¼ cup spring water
- 1 tbsp sea salt

- 1 tbsp onion powder
- ½ tsp cayenne pepper powder
- ½ tsp ground ginger
- 1 tbsp liquid smoke
- Grapeseed oil for frying

Directions:

1. In a bowl, combine all the ingredients, minus the grapeseed oil. In the refrigerator, let the zucchini strips marinate for at least two hours.
2. On your Instant Pot, turn the sauté setting to high and heat the oil until it begins to slightly smoke. Fry the marinated zucchini strips until crisp, about 3 minutes per side.

Nutritional Information: Calories 72; Fat 3g; Sodium 54mg; Carbs 10.6g; Fiber 2g; Sugar 7g; Protein 2.3g

Sesame Spelt Bread

Preparation time: 8 minutes
Cooking time: 6 hours
Serves: 8
Ingredients:
- 4-½ cups spelt flour
- 2 tsp sea salt
- 2 cups spring water
- ¼ cup agave
- Grapeseed oil for brushing the bread
- A dash of sesame seeds

Directions:

1. To combine the ingredients, use the mixer's hook attachment. Combine the salt and spelt flour in a bowl. 10 seconds of mixing should be done in a mixer. Add the water and agave next. To create a

dough, mix for ten minutes or longer.

2. Place the dough in a clean bowl after coating it with grapeseed oil. Give yourself at least an hour to rest. After that, line the Instant Pot's base with parchment paper.

3. Before placing the dough inside the Instant Pot, sprinkle it with sesame seeds. Although the vent should not be in the sealing position, close the lid.

4. Select "Slow Cook" and set the cooking period to six hours.

Nutritional Information: Calories 150; Fat 0.9g; Sodium 584mg; Carbs 30.5g; Fiber 1.3g; Sugar 0.2g; Protein 4.2g

Veggie Quiche

Preparation time: 14 minutes
Cooking time: 4 hours
Serves: 4
Ingredients:
- 1 cup garbanzos bean flour
- ¾ cup fresh coconut milk
- 1 tbsp sea salt
- 1 tbsp oregano
- ¼ tsp cayenne pepper
- 2 cups mushrooms, sliced
- 1 cup kale, chopped
- ½ cup white onions, chopped
- ½ cup yellow peppers, seeded and chopped

Directions:
1. Combine the coconut milk, salt, oregano, and cayenne pepper with the garbanzo bean flour. Create a smooth dough by mixing.
2. Combine the remaining ingredients. Pour the ingredients into the Instant Pot's bottom-mounted parchment paper pan. Although the

vent should not be in the sealing position, close the lid.

3. Select the slow cooker setting and set the timer for 4 hours.

Nutritional Information: Calories 233; Fat 4.7g; Sodium 519mg; Carbs 37g; Fiber 7g; Sugar 8g; Protein 12g

Savory Tomato-Bean Soup

Preparation time: 15 minutes

Cooking time: 1 hour 20 minutes

Serves: 6 to 8

Ingredients:

- 10 chopped plum tomatoes
- 1 chopped tomatillo
- 3 cups cooked garbanzo beans
- ½ cup chopped red bell pepper
- ½ cup minced onions
- ½ cup chopped green bell pepper
- 2 tsp onion powder
- 1 tsp cayenne powder
- 1 tsp sweet basil
- 1 tsp oregano
- ½ tsp achiote
- 2 tsp pure sea salt
- 2 tsp grapeseed oil
- spring water, to cook
- sausage, for serving

Directions:

1. In a large pot, combine bell pepper, grapeseed oil, onions, and tomatillos. Cook the vegetables on medium heat for 4 to 5 minutes.

2. Fill the stockpot with the garbanzo beans, spices, tomatoes, and spring water. Stir and heat until boiling. For about an hour, simmer the tomato-bean mixture. occasionally stir. If desired, add sliced

sausage links a few minutes before the soup is done cooking. Serve the soup and savor it!

Nutritional Information: Calories 87; Fat 1.6g; Sodium 217mg; Carbs 18.8g; Fiber 2.4g; Sugar 14.5g; Protein 1.4g

Clam and Vegetable Chowder

Preparation time: 5 minutes
Cooking time: 40 minutes
Serves: 6 to 8
Ingredients:
- 1 ½ cups cooked garbanzo beans
- 1 ½ cups chopped oyster mushrooms
- 2 cups garbanzo bean flour
- 1 cup mashed white onions
- ½ cup chopped butternut squash
- ½ cup medium diced kale
- 1 cup homemade hempseed milk
- 1 cup aquafaba
- 2 tsp dill
- ½ tsp cayenne powder
- 2 tsp basil
- 1 tbsp pure sea salt
- 1 tbsp grapeseed oil
- 7 cups spring water

Directions:

1. Combine 6 cups of spring water and aquafaba in a big saucepan.
2. Add half of each spice to the saucepan along with the cooked garbanzo beans, diced veggies, and beans.
3. After that, combine them, bring to a boil, and simmer for 10 minutes at medium heat while stirring regularly.

4. In another dish, combine the hempseed milk, grapeseed oil, 1 cup of spring water, and the remaining spices.
5. Whisk in the chickpea flour gradually.
6. Continue adding the flour and whisking continually until the mixture is completely smooth and lump-free. Whisk the mixture to prevent lumps before adding it gradually to the saucepan of veggies. Cook the chopped oyster mushrooms for 10 minutes over low heat. sometimes stir the soup. Your vegan clam chowder is ready; eat some!

Nutritional Information: Calories 339; Fat 7g; Sodium 431mg; Carbs 53g; Fiber 11g; Sugar 12g; Protein 17.5g

Zucchini-Banana Bread Pancakes

Preparation time: 10 minutes
Cooking time: 40 minutes
Serves: 4
Ingredients:
- 1 cup minced zucchini
- 2 cups spelt flour
- ¼ cup pureed burro bananas
- ½ cup chopped walnuts
- 2 tbsp date sugar
- 1 tbsp grapeseed oil
- 2 cups homemade walnut milk

Directions:

1. Place the spelt flour and date sugar in a sizable bowl. Stir everything thoroughly. Put homemade walnut milk and pureed burro bananas in the bowl. Stir the ingredients together thoroughly to avoid lumps.
2. Combine the other ingredients in the bowl with the chopped walnuts and the minced zucchini. On medium heat, warm a skillet

pan with grapeseed oil. To make the pancakes, pour some prepared zucchini batter into the pan. For each side of the pancakes, cook them for about 5 minutes.

Nutritional Information: Calories 348; Fat 16.6g; Sodium 62mg; Carbs 29g; Fiber 8g; Sugar 14.6g; Protein 26g

Avocado Tomato Pasta

Preparation time: 5 minutes
Cooking time: 20 minutes
Serves: 4

Ingredients:

- 4 cups cooked spelt pasta
- 1 medium diced avocado
- 2 cups halved cherry tomatoes
- 1 minced fresh basil
- 1 tsp agave syrup
- 1 tbsp key lime juice
- ¼ cup olive oil

Directions:

1. Put the cooked pasta in the appropriate bowl.
2. Diced avocado, cherry tomatoes , and basil are all added to the dish. All the components should be well mixed.
3. In another bowl, combine the key lime juice, olive oil, agave syrup, and sea salt.

4. The paste should be well mixed with the liquid once it has been whisked in. Please, spaghetti with basil and avocado!

Nutritional Information: Calories 465; Fat 23g; Sodium 17mg; Carbs 60g; Fiber 11.8g; Sugar 8g; Protein 12g

Awesome White Sandwich Bread

Preparation time: 9 minutes
Cooking time: 50 minutes
Serves: 16

Ingredients:

- 1 cup warm water
- 2 tbsp active dry yeast
- 4 tbsp oil
- 2 ½ tsp salt
- 2 tbsp raw sugar or 4 tbsp maple syrup/agave nectar
- 1 cup warm almond milk or any other non-dairy milk of your choice
- 6 cups all-purpose flour

Directions:

1. Combine yeast, sugar, and warm water in a bowl. A good stir for 5 minutes or until a little foam forms is required for setting.
2. Fill a good mixing bowl with the flour and salt. Good stirring
3. Combine the milk, oil, and yeast mixture into a dough. Each time you need to add water to get a smooth, non-sticky dough, do it gently and thoroughly. or, if necessary, add extra flour.

4. Using your hands or a mixer, knead the dough until it is soft and malleable.
5. Mist the dough with water.
6. Fill a basin with the dough. It should be covered with a cloth and left until it doubles in size.
7. Next, place the dough on a spotless, level surface. Roll out the dough.
8. Use parchment paper to line a loaf pan. If you'd rather, lubricate with some oil. Put it in a loaf pan.
9. Spray the dough with extra water, then cover it with a towel once more. Wait until the dough has doubled in bulk.
10. Cook for 40 to 50 minutes at 370°F in a preheated oven.

11. After cooling, slice into 16 equal pieces and use as needed. Store in a breadbox at room temperature.

Nutritional Information: Calories 226; Fat 4g; Sodium 195mg; Carbs 41g; Fiber 1.7g; Sugar 4.5g; Protein 5.6g

Coconut Barley Porridge

Preparation time: 8 minutes
Cooking time: 5 minutes
Serves: 2
Ingredients:
- 1 cup unsweetened coconut milk, divided
- 1 small banana, peeled and sliced
- ½ cup barley
- 3 drops liquid stevia
- ¼ cup coconuts, chopped

Directions:

1. In a bowl, thoroughly combine the barley, stevia, and half the coconut milk. For about 6 hours, cover and chill.
2. In a saucepan, combine the barley mixture with the coconut milk. 5 minutes of cooking at medium heat.
3. Add banana slices and coconut shavings on top. Serve.

Nutritional Information: Calories 336; Fat 8g; Sodium 68mg; Carbs 59g; Fiber 10g; Sugar 13.4g; Protein 9.7g

Low-Carb Blueberry Smoothie

Preparation time: 5 minutes
Cooking time: None
Serves: 3
Ingredients:

- 14 ounces canned unsweetened coconut milk
- ½ cup unsweetened almond milk
- ½ cup blueberries (fresh or frozen)
- 4 tablespoons pea protein powder
- ½ teaspoon vanilla extract

Directions:

1. Fill a high-speed blender with the blueberries, almond milk, pea protein powder, and vanilla.
2. Add the coconut milk gradually based on the consistency of the smoothie you want.
3. Blend on high until all the ingredients are thoroughly combined and the smoothie has turned a light purple.

4. You can keep your baby in the refrigerator for three to four days in a sealed container.

Nutritional Information: Calories 320; Fat 29.5g; Sodium 37mg; Carbs 11.4g; Fiber 2g; Sugar 5g; Protein 7.4g

Make-Ahead Smoothie

Preparation time: 10 minutes
Cooking time: 2 minutes
Serves: 5

Ingredients:
- 2 ½ cups whole strawberries, blueberries, raspberries, or chopped mango, divided
- 2 ½ cups sliced banana, divided
- 5 cups unsweetened vanilla almond milk or soymilk, divided

Directions:

1. Add the blueberries, almond milk, pea protein powder, and vanilla to a high-speed blender.

2. Depending on the desired smoothie consistency, gradually add the coconut milk.

3. Blend on high until the smoothie is well incorporated and has developed a light purple color.
4. If you place your infant in a sealed container, you may keep him or her in the fridge for three to four days.

Nutritional Information: Calories 163; Fat 2.3g; Sodium 118mg; Carbs 31g; Fiber 4g; Sugar 19g; Protein 7g

Strawberry-Kiwifruit Smoothies

Preparation time: 5 minutes
Cooking time: 2 minutes
Serves: 8
Ingredients:
- 4 cups sliced fresh strawberries
- 1 medium banana, sliced
- 1 (6-ounce) container vanilla low-fat yogurt
- 1 cup ice cubes
- 1 kiwifruit, peeled and sliced, optional

Directions:
1. Combine strawberries, banana, and yogurt in a blender; cover and process until smooth. Blend until smooth while adding ice cubes one at a time through the lid's hole while the blender is running. Into 8 small glasses, pour. Kiwifruit can be used as a garnish if desired; serve right away.
Nutritional Information: Calories 61; Fat 0.7g; Sodium 17mg; Carbs 13g; Fiber 2.4g; Sugar 8.5g; Protein 2g

Carrot Cantaloupe Smoothie Bowl

Preparation time: 15 minutes
Cooking time: 2 minutes
Serves: 6

Ingredients:

- 4 cups frozen cubed cantaloupe (½-inch pieces)
- ¾ cup carrot juice
- Pinch of salt
- Melon balls, berries, nuts, or fresh basil for garnish

Directions:

1. Combine canned fruit, juice, and salt in a food processor or high-speed blender. Alternate between pulsing and blending for one to two minutes, pausing occasionally to stir and scrape the sides as necessary to keep the mixture thick and smooth.
2. If desired, top the smoothe with additional melon, berries, nuts, or basil before serving.

Nutritional Information: Calories 289; Fat 1.5g; Sodium 994mg; Carbs 68.7g; Fiber 7g; Sugar 57g; Protein 7g

Berry-Spinach Smoothies

Preparation time: 15 minutes
Cooking time: 2 minutes
Serves: 8

Ingredients:

- 2 cups frozen unsweetened strawberries
- 1 cup frozen unsweetened raspberries
- 1 cup fresh blackberries or blueberries
- 1 cup fresh baby spinach leaves
- 1 cup pomegranate juice

- 3 tbsp sugar-free vanilla-flavor protein powder, soy protein powder or nonfat dry milk powder

Directions:

1. Blend strawberries, raspberries, blackberries, pineapple, pomegranate juice, and protein powder in a blender. Blend under cover until smooth. Pour into serving glasses.

Nutritional Information: Calories 80; Fat 0.5g; Sodium 8mg; Carbs 18.6g; Fiber 2.8g; Sugar 14.7g; Protein 1.8g

Berry-Banana Smoothie with Almonds

Preparation time: 4 minutes
Cooking time: 20 minutes
Serves: 4
Ingredients:
- ⅔ cup frozen raspberries
- ½ cup frozen sliced banana
- ½ cup plain unsweetened almond milk
- 5 tablespoons sliced almonds, divided
- ¼ tsp ground cinnamon
- ⅛ tsp ground cardamom
- ⅛ teaspoon vanilla extract
- ¼ cup blueberries
- 1 tbsp unsweetened coconut flakes

Directions:

1. In a blender, combine raspberries, banana, almond milk, 3 tbsp of almonds, cinnamon, cardamom, and vanilla, and process until extremely smooth.
2. Place the smoothed mixture in a bowl and top with the remaining 2 tbsp of almonds, coconut, and blueberries.

Nutritional Information: Calories 129; Fat 2.6g; Sodium 44mg; Carbs 25.7g; Fiber 3g; Sugar 19.4g; Protein 2.6g

Cauliflower-Melon Smoothies

Preparation time: 8 minutes
Cooking time: 15 minutes
Serves: 2

Ingredients:

- 1 cup coarsely chopped fresh cauliflower
- 2 cups honeydew melon, cut into 1-inch cubes
- 2 cups cucumber, cut into 1-inch pieces
- ½ cup lightly packed fresh mint leaves
- ¼ cup water
- 2 tablespoons honey
- 1 cup ice cubes

Directions:

1. Cook the cauliflower, uncovered, in a small saucepan with enough boiling water to cover it for 10 to 12 minutes or until very tender. Drain. To quickly cool, rinse with cold water and drain one more time.
2. Add the following ingredients to a blender in that order: honeydew melon, cauliflower, cumin, mint, water, and honey. Cover and mix until very smooth, stopping and scraping the blender's sides as necessary. Add cubes of ice. Cover and combine until smooth. Pour into glasses and serve right away.
3. Go to an upright freezer container. To freeze for up to six months, cover.

4. Thaw smoothies in the refrigerator before serving. Stir well before serving.

Nutritional Information: Calories 112; Fat 1g; Sodium 47mg; Carbs 25.5g; Fiber 4.3g; Sugar 21g; Protein 3.3g

Simple Lime Watercress Salad

Preparation time: 5 minutes
Cooking time: 5 minutes
Serves: 2

Ingredients:
- 2 cups torn watercress
- ½ cucumber, sliced
- 1 tbsp key lime juice
- 2 tbsp olive oil
- pure sea salt, to taste
- cayenne powder, to taste

Directions:

1. Olive oil and key lime juice should be added to a salad dish. Then, thoroughly blend them.
2. Slice the cucumber, then add all of the slices to the bowl. Add watercress to the bowl after tearing it.
3. As desired, add cayenne pepper and pure sea salt on top. Completely combine. Enjoy this fast salad for detox!

Nutritional Information: Calories 125; Fat 13.5g; Sodium 14mg; Carbs 1g; Fiber 0.2g; Sugar 0.2g; Protein 0.8g

Kale and Sweet Potato Hash

Preparation time: 10 minutes
Cooking time: 15 minutes
Serves: 2

Ingredients:
- 1 tsp avocado oil
- 2 cups peeled and cubed sweet potatoes

- ½ cup chopped kale
- ½ cup diced onion
- ½ tsp sea salt
- ½ tsp freshly ground black pepper
- ½ avocado, cubed (optional)
- 1 to 2 tsp sesame seeds or hemp seeds (optional)

Directions:

1. Heat the avocado oil in a large skillet over medium heat. When the sweet potatoes are soft, add the kale, onion, salt, and pepper and sauté for 10 to 15 minutes. Get rid of the heat.
2. Transfer to 1 large or 2 small plates and serve after gently incorporating the avocado and sesame seeds (if using).

Nutritional Information: Calories 143; Fat 10.7g; Sodium 397mg; Carbs 12g; Fiber 6.4g; Sugar 2g; Protein 2.8g

Apple Pumpkin Smoothie

Preparation time: 15 minutes
Cooking time: 5 minutes
Serves: 4

Ingredients:
- 1 ½ cups unsweetened vanilla almond milk
- 1 ⅓ cups chopped apples (2 medium)
- ½ (15-ounce) can pumpkin
- ¾ cup plain nonfat Greek yogurt
- ½ cup ice
- 2 tbsp maple syrup
- ¼ teaspoon pumpkin pie spice
- ⅛ teaspoon salt
- ¼ cup high-protein honey-almond-flavor granola, such as Bear Naked brand

Directions:

1. Blend almond milk, almonds, pumpkin, yogurt, ice, maple syrup, pumpkin pie spice, and salt in a blender. Cover and combine until smooth.
2. Sprinkle 1 tbsp of the granola on top of each serving.

Nutritional Information: Calories 209; Fat 6.4g; Sodium 203mg; Carbs 35g; Fiber 2g; Sugar 26g; Protein 5g

Orange-Carrot Smoothie

Preparation time: 15 minutes
Cooking time: 20 minutes
Serves: 2
Ingredients:
- 1 cup sliced carrots
- ½ teaspoon finely shredded orange peel
- 1 cup orange juice
- 1 ½ cups ice cubes
- 3 (1 inch) pieces orange peel curls

Directions:

1. Cook the carrots in a small amount of boiling water in a covered small saucepan for about 15 minutes, or until they are very tender. good drainage canal.
2. Put the drained carrots in the blender. Add freshly squeezed orange juice and orange peel. Cover and combine until smooth. Include the ice cubes, cover, and blend until smooth. Pour into glasses. Begin with orange peel curls if desired.

Nutritional Information: Calories 167; Fat 0.8g; Sodium 87mg; Carbs 39g; Fiber 4.5g; Sugar 26.6g; Protein 3g

Vegan Chocolate Smoothie

Preparation time: 10 minutes
Cooking time: None
Serves: 1

Ingredients:

- ½ ripe avocado
- 3 tablespoons cocoa powder
- 1 cup full-fat coconut milk
- ½ cup water
- 1 teaspoon lime juice
- pinch mineral salt
- 6-7 drops liquid Stevia
- Fresh mint (for decoration)

Directions:

1. Place all the ingredients in a blender.
2. Puree at a high speed until smooth and creamy. Add more liquid stevia, if desired, to taste.
3. If desired, garnish with fresh mint and serve.

Nutritional Information: Calories 748; Fat 72.7g; Sodium 859mg; Carbs 31g; Fiber 13.7g; Sugar 9g; Protein 8.6g

Almond Butter Chocolate Shake

Preparation time: 8 minutes
Cooking time: None
Serves: 1

Ingredients:

- 1 ½ cup full fat coconut milk or substitute half and half
- 2 tbsp almond butter
- 2 tablespoons cocoa powder
- 1 ½ tablespoons monk fruit sweetener or more, depending on taste

- ½ teaspoon vanilla extract

Directions:

1. Fill a blender with all the ingredients.

2. Puree on high until it's creamy and smooth. Depending on flavor, if needed, add additional liquid stevia.

3. Add fresh mint as a garnish, if desired, and then serve.

Nutritional Information: Calories 236; Fat 20g; Sodium 17mg; Carbs 11g; Fiber 4.8g; Sugar 2g; Protein 7.6g

Vegan and Vegetarian Recipes

Vanilla Mug Brownie

Preparation time: 10 minutes
Cooking time: 1 minutes
Serves: 1
Ingredients:
- ¼ cup whole wheat flour
- 2 tsp white sugar, or to taste
- 2 tsp unsweetened cocoa powder
- ¼ tsp baking soda
- 1 pinch salt
- ¼ cup water
- 2 tbsp canola oil
- ⅛ tsp vanilla extract
- 2 tsp vegan chocolate chips (such as Enjoy Life®)

Directions:

1. In a cup that can be microwaved, combine whole wheat flour, white sugar, cocoa powder, baking soda, and salt. Add the canola oil, vanilla essence, and water. Add the chocolate chunks and stir.
2. Cook in the microwave for 50 to 1 minute, or until well done.

Nutritional Information: Calories 496; Fat 35g; Sodium 793mg; Carbs 44g; Fiber 4.8g; Sugar 13g; Protein 5.8g

Savory Almond Paste

Preparation time: 10 minutes
Cooking time: 15 minutes
Serves: 3
Ingredients:

- 1 cup blanched whole almonds
- ½ cup white sugar plus 1 tbsp
- ¼ cup water
- ⅛ tsp almond extract

Directions:

1. In a food processor, blend the almonds until they resemble meal, scraping the sides and the bottom of the bowl as necessary. Don't overprocess it; at this stage, the mixture should still be crumbly rather than paste-like.
2. In a small saucepan, combine 12 cups plus 1 tbsp of sugar with water. up to a boil.
3. Next, boil the mixture for 4 minutes at medium heat. Heat it for a further 6 to 8 minutes, or until it reaches 240°F and becomes a medium-thick syrup. The syrup will thicken as it cools if you overcook it.

4. Next, switch off the heat. Add the almonds and almond essence, and combine.
5. Turn the heat back on and cook the almond paste for 30 to 60 seconds, or until it holds together, stirring with a spatula and scraping the bottom and sides to prevent burning.
6. Turn off the heat under the pan. Use right away if it is cold enough to handle, or wrap in waxed paper and store in an airtight container for up to a few weeks. Alternatively, you may freeze the wrapped almond paste for up to six months by placing it in a freezer bag.

Nutritional Information: Calories 983; Fat 47.5g; Sodium 3mg; Carbs 133g; Fiber 12g; Sugar 117g; Protein 20g

Chocolate Zucchini Brownies

Preparation time: 10 minutes
Cooking time: 30 minutes

Serves: 2
Ingredients:
- cooking spray
- 1 cup white sugar
- ½ cup brown sugar
- ½ cup olive oil
- 1 tbsp of vanilla extract
- 2 cups all-purpose flour
- ½ cup cocoa powder (such as Hershey's®)
- 1 ½ tsp baking soda
- 1 tsp salt
- 3 cups shredded zucchini 1 cup vegan chocolate chips

Directions:

1. Carefully preheat the oven to 350° F. Apply cooking spray to a baking pan that will work.

2. Combine the sugar, brown sugar, and olive oil in a large mixing bowl and beat with an electric mixer until well combined. Add the vanilla essence and combine. Mix the flour, baking soda, salt, and cocoa powder well. It will be a dry mixture.

3. Using a spoon, thoroughly incorporate the zucchini into the mixture. Give the mixture five minutes to become more wet. Add the vegan chocolate chips and stir. Fill the prepared pan with the batter.

4. Bake for approximately 25 to 30 minutes, or until the top is dry and the edges start to pull away from the pan's sides. Before cutting, let complete cooling occur.

Nutritional Information: Calories 1656; Fat 63g; Sodium 2161mg; Carbs 269g; Fiber 13.7g; Sugar 158g; Protein 21g

Chocolate Mug Cake

Preparation time: 10 minutes

Cooking time: 5 minutes
Serves: 1

Ingredients:

- 4 tbsp all-purpose flour
- 3 tbsp white sugar
- 2 tbsp unsweetened cocoa powder
- ¼ tsp baking powder
- 4 tbsp applesauce
- 3 tbsp soy milk
- 1 tbsp vegan chocolate chips, or more to taste
- 1 tbsp toasted flaked coconut (optional)

Directions:

1. In a cup, mash together the flour, sugar, cocoa powder, and baking powder. In a another bowl, combine the soy milk and applesauce; add to the flour mixture. Stir well to combine. Add the chocolate chunks and coconut on top after folding.
2. Heat in the microwave for 3 minutes on high, or until the mug cake is properly risen and set.

Nutritional Information: Calories 460; Fat 10.8g; Sodium 168mg; Carbs 88.6g; Fiber 6g; Sugar 43g; Protein 9g

Vegan Jalapeno Poppers and Mushrooms

Preparation time: 10 minutes
Cooking time: 30 minutes
Serves: 2

Ingredients:

- 1 tbsp vegetable oil
- 12 medium jalapeno peppers
- 1 (8 ounces) package button mushrooms, finely diced
- ½ cup finely diced onion
- 2 cloves garlic, minced

- 1 (8 ounces) tub vegan cream cheese substitute, softened
- 1 cup vegan shredded cheese substitute, divided
- salt and ground black pepper to taste

Directions:

1. Split the pepper in half after removing the seeds.
2. Carefully preheat the oven to 375°F. Place the jalapeo halves on a baking sheet covered with aluminum foil, open side up.
3. Put the vegetable oil in a pan and heat it up over medium-high heat.

4. Add the mushrooms, onion, and garlic, and sauté for 8 minutes, or until the mushrooms are tender and have released their liquid. To absorb any excess liquid, move the vegetables to a dish lined with paper towels.
5. In a mixing bowl, combine the mushroom mixture, fake cream cheese, 1/4 cup fake shredded cheese, salt, and pepper. On the baking sheet, spoon the mixture into the jalapeo pepper halves.
6. Bake for approximately 20 minutes, or until well done, in the oven that has been preheated.
7. Take it out of the oven.
8. Sprinkle the top with the remaining 1/4 cup of the cheese replacement.
9. After that, broil the dish in the hot oven for one to two minutes, or until the cheese is melted and gently browned.

Nutritional Information: Calories 865; Fat 29g; Sodium 1184mg; Carbs 137g; Fiber 16g; Sugar 48.6g; Protein 32g

Brown Lentils

Preparation time: 8 minutes
Cooking time: 10 minutes
Serves: 4

Ingredients:
- 1 cup brown or green lentils, rinsed well and drained
- 1 ¾ cups filtered water
- ½ tsp sea salt
- ¼ tsp black pepper

Directions:

1. Fill the base of a 6-quart pressure cooker with the rinsed lentils and water. Season with salt and pepper.
2. Secure the lid, then set the timer for 10 minutes at maximum pressure. After the cooking is finished, let the pressure fall naturally for about 10 minutes. Use the quick release to release any remaining pressure after that.
3. Whether hot or at room temperature, serve the lentils.

Nutritional Information: Calories 169; Fat 0.5g; Sodium 294mg; Carbs 30.5g; Fiber 5.2g; Sugar 1g; Protein 11.84g

Basil-Spinach Lasagna

Preparation time: 15 minutes
Cooking time: 50 minutes
Serves: 8

Ingredients:
- 2 tbsp olive oil
- 1 ½ cup chopped onion
- 3 tbsp minced garlic
- 4 (14.5 ounces) cans stewed tomatoes
- ⅓ cup tomato paste
- ½ cup chopped fresh basil
- ½ cup chopped parsley
- 1 tsp salt
- 1 tsp ground black pepper

- 1 (16 ounces) package lasagna noodles
- 2 pounds firm tofu
- 2 tbsp minced garlic
- ¼ cup chopped fresh basil
- ¼ cup chopped parsley
- ½ tsp salt
- ground black pepper to taste
- 3 (10 ounces) packages frozen chopped spinach, thawed and drained

Directions:

To make the tomato sauce:

1. To create the sauce, have a large, heavy saucepan ready and heat the olive oil over medium heat.

2. In the saucepan, sauté the onions for 5 minutes, or until they are soft. Add the garlic and cook for another five minutes.

3. In a saucepan, mix the tomatoes, tomato paste, basil, and parsley. Salt and pepper the sauce, give it a good stir, turn the heat down to low, and cover it for an hour.

4. While the sauce is simmering, bring a large saucepan of salted water to a boil. The lasagna noodles should be boiled for nine minutes, drained, and well rinsed.

5. Carefully preheat the oven to 400° F.

6. Combine all of the tofu blocks in a large mixing bowl. In a mixing bowl, combine the parsley, basil, and garlic. Squeeze the tofu pieces with your fingers to combine everything after adding the salt and pepper. Completely combine.

To make the lasagna:

1. A 9x13 inch casserole dish should have 1 cup of tomato sauce on the bottom. One layer of lasagna noodles should be placed, followed by one-third of the tofu mixture.

2. On top of the tofu, evenly distribute the spinach.

3. Place another layer of noodles on top of the tofu, then add 1 and a half cups of tomato sauce.

4. After that, add another third of the tofu mixture on top of the noodles, cover with 1 1/2 cups of tomato sauce, then top with one more layer of noodles.
5. Then, top the noodles with 13 of the tofu and the remaining tomato sauce.
6. For 30 minutes, bake the lasagna with foil covering.
7. Serve right away and delight in.

Nutritional Information: Calories 377; Fat 17.7g; Sodium 1043mg; Carbs 34g; Fiber 12.7g; Sugar 10.7g; Protein 30g

Mayo Mushroom Sandwich

Preparation time: 10 minutes
Cooking time: 15 minutes
Serves: 2
Ingredients:
- ½ cup vegan Worcestershire sauce
- ½ cup tamari soy sauce
- ½ cup water
- 1 shiitake mushroom
- 1 tbsp fermented black bean paste
- 1 tbsp minced shallot
- 1 clove garlic, crushed
- 1 strip nori seaweed
- 4 ½ ounces tempeh
- ¼ cup vegan mayonnaise
- 1 tsp sriracha sauce
- 1 (6 inches) French baguette, sliced into bite-sized cubes
- 1 tbsp olive oil
- 1 jalapeno pepper, sliced
- ½ ounce pickled daikon, or to taste
- ½ ounce pickled carrot, or to taste

- 2 cucumbers, sliced to taste
- 3 tbsp chopped fresh cilantro

Directions:

1. Carefully preheat the oven to 350°F. Next, line a baking sheet with parchment paper.

2. Place a pot over medium heat and add the Worcestershire sauce, tamari, Worcestershire sauce, water, mushrooms, black bean paste, shallot, garlic clove, and seaweed. Immediately turn off the heat and let it cool. Remove the sauce from the pan after discarding the sediments.

3. In a bowl, mix the tempeh with 1/3 cup of the sauce. Tempeh should be marinated for 20 minutes, turning it halfway through.

4. On another plate, combine 1 tsp of the tempeh marinade, vegan mayo, and sriracha. Keep refrigerated until ready to use.

5. Arrange the baguette slices on the baking sheet that has been oiled and drizzle with olive oil. Place the bread in a single layer after tossing it.

6. Bake in a preheated oven for 15 minutes. About 8 minutes longer of cooking are required to brown the bread. Transfer to a bowl for mixing.

7. Set the liquid aside and arrange the tempeh on a baking sheet. The leftover marinade should be basted halfway through the ten minutes of baking. Continue baking for 10 more minutes, basting halfway through.

8. Cut the tempeh into cubes. Bread, tempeh, chopped jalapenos, pickled daikon, carrots, cucumbers, and cilantro should be placed in serving bowls. Top with Sriracha mayo when serving.

Nutritional Information: Calories 612; Fat 27g; Sodium 6404mg; Carbs 71g; Fiber 6g; Sugar 17g; Protein 28g

Lemony Vanilla Cake

Preparation time: 10 minutes
Cooking time: 35 minutes
Serves: 2

Ingredients:
- 1 cup plain soy milk
- 1 tbsp apple cider vinegar
- 1 ½ cups unbleached all-purpose flour
- 1 cup white sugar
- 1 tsp baking soda
- 1 tsp baking powder
- ½ tsp salt
- ⅓ cup canola oil
- ¼ cup water
- 1 tbsp lemon juice
- 1 tbsp vanilla extract
- ¼ tsp almond extract

Directions:

1. Carefully preheat the oven to 350°F. 8x8-inch greased and dusted baking dish

2. In a proper measuring cup made of glass, combine the soy milk and vinegar.

3. In a mixing bowl, combine the sugar, baking soda, flour, baking powder, and salt.

4. With a fork, quickly blend the soy milk mixture with the canola oil, water, lemon juice, vanilla, and almond extracts. Once the batter is lump-free, add the soy milk mixture. The prepared baking dish should now be filled with the batter.

5. Bake the cake for 35 minutes or longer; a toothpick inserted in the center of the cake should come out clean.

Nutritional Information: Calories 935; Fat 39g; Sodium 1285mg; Carbs 130.5g; Fiber 2.6g; Sugar 56.7g; Protein 11.7g

Awesome Mushroom Stroganoff

Preparation time: 10 minutes

Cooking time: 15 minutes
Serves: 1
Ingredients:
- 8 ounces oyster mushrooms
- 1 tbsp oil, or to taste
- 1 small onion, diced
- 1 tbsp all-purpose flour
- 1 cup almond milk
- 1 tbsp lemon juice
- salt and ground black pepper to taste

Directions:

1. Shred the mushrooms with a fork.
2. Place a skillet on the stove and turn the heat to medium-high. The oil is then heated.
3. Include the mushrooms and onion and cook for 2 to 3 minutes, or until the vegetables are soft. While stirring, add the flour and simmer for a little while.

4. In a mixing dish, combine almond milk and lemon juice. For 7 to 8 minutes, cook. To taste, add salt and pepper to the food.

Nutritional Information: Calories 989; Fat 19g; Sodium 206mg; Carbs 211g; Fiber 29g; Sugar 31.7g; Protein 26g

Vegan Au Gratin Potatoes

Preparation time: 10 minutes
Cooking time: 20 minutes
Serves: 6
Ingredients:
- 6 large potatoes, peeled and cubed
- 1 ¼ cups vegetable broth, divided

- 2 tbsp all-purpose flour
- 1 tsp seasoning salt
- ½ tsp ground black pepper
- ¼ tsp dry mustard
- 1 cup soft bread crumbs
- ⅛ tsp nutmeg
- 2 cups soy milk
- 1 ½ cups Cheddar-flavored soy cheese, shredded and divided
- 3 tsp paprika

Directions:

1. Carefully preheat the oven to 350°F.
2. Combine nutmeg, mustard, flour, pepper, and seasoning salt in a small mixing dish. Mix thoroughly.
3. Add salted water to a big pot. Add the potatoes after bringing all the ingredients to a boil.

4. Boil the potatoes for approximately 15 minutes, or until they are cooked but firm. After draining, put the food in a 9 x 13-inch baking dish.
5. In the meantime, heat up two tbsp of broth in a little pot. Reduce the heat to low.
6. In the saucepan, stir in the nutmeg-mustard combination.
7. Add soy milk gradually while stirring constantly until the mixture thickens. Add the soy cheese in two batches. To melt the cheese, continually stir. apply to potatoes.
8. In a small mixing bowl, combine the bread crumbs and the remaining broth.
9. Spoon over the potatoes evenly. Add the remaining soy cheese over top. Add paprika to the mixture.
10. Bake for 20 minutes in a preheated oven.

Nutritional Information: Calories 495; Fat 13g; Sodium 823mg; Carbs 76.8g; Fiber 9g; Sugar 7g; Protein 19g

Baked Vegan Pancakes

Preparation time: 10 minutes
Cooking time: 15 minutes
Serves: 1

Ingredients:

- 1 ¼ cups all-purpose flour
- 2 tbsp white sugar
- 2 tsp baking powder
- ½ tsp salt
- 1¼ cups water
- 1 tbsp oil

Directions:

1. Sift the flour, sugar, baking powder, and salt together in a large mixing bowl; create a well in the center.
2. In a different bowl, thoroughly whisk the water and oil.
3. After that, pour into the flour amalgam. There will be lumps in the mixture; stir just until combined.

4. Heat a griddle that has been lightly greased over medium-high heat.
5. Spoon large amounts of batter onto the griddle. Cook until bubbles form and the edges are completely dried.
6. Cook again for 1 to 2 minutes, or until the bottoms are browned. Continue by using the remaining batter.

Nutritional Information: Calories 760; Fat 15g; Sodium 1181mg; Carbs 140g; Fiber 4.4g; Sugar 16g; Protein 16g

Herbed Irish Stew

Preparation time: 10 minutes

Cooking time: 15 minutes
Serves: 8
Ingredients:

- ¼ cup extra-virgin olive oil
- 3 leeks, thinly sliced
- 1 cup chopped red potatoes
- 1 cup peeled and sliced parsnips
- 1 cup peeled and chopped turnip
- 1 cup sliced celery
- 1 cup sliced carrots
- 4 cups garbanzo beans, drained
- 4 cups low-sodium vegetable broth
- 2 cups vegan stout beer (such as Samuel Smith's)
- ½ cup chopped fresh parsley
- ¼ tsp dried rosemary
- ¼ tsp dried thyme
- ¼ tsp dried marjoram
- ¼ cup water (optional)
- salt and ground black pepper to taste

Directions:

1. Place the right pot on the stove and turn the heat to medium-high. Heat it up after adding the olive oil. Leeks should be cooked for 3 to 5 minutes or until translucent.
2. Include potatoes, parsnips, turnips, celery, and carrots. 4 minutes of cooking and stirring, or until slightly soft and coated with oil.
3. Optional ingredients include parsley, vegetable broth, garbanzo beans, and beer. The stew should boil.

4. Continue cooking the mixture for another hour or two, or until the vegetables are tender and the stew has considerably thickened. Insert the herbs. Add a splash of water if necessary; season with salt and pepper to taste.

Nutritional Information: Calories 168; Fat 2.3g; Sodium 526mg; Carbs 33g; Fiber 7g; Sugar 10g; Protein 5.9g

Mayo Vegan Coleslaw

Preparation time: 10 minutes plus 2 hours for chilling
Cooking time: 15 minutes
Serves: 2

Ingredients:

- 1 (16 ounces) bag coleslaw mix
- ⅔ cup vegan mayonnaise (such as Follow Your Heart® Vegenaise®)
- ½ cup granular sucralose sweetener (such as Splenda®)
- 3 tbsp olive oil
- 1 tbsp white vinegar
- 1 tbsp poppy seeds
- ¼ tsp salt

Directions:

1. In a good mixing bowl, add the cole slaw mix and well blend.
2. In a small mixing bowl, combine vegan mayonnaise, sweetener, olive oil, vinegar, poppy seeds, and salt. Fold the slaw mixture into the dressing gradually.
3. The coleslaw should be chilled for at least two hours before serving. Offer cold.

Nutritional Information: Calories 521; Fat 48g; Sodium 1013mg; Carbs 16g; Fiber 6g; Sugar 3g; Protein 9g

Gingerbread Cookies

Preparation time: 10 minutes plus 2 hours for refrigerating
Cooking time: 15 minutes
Serves: 1

Ingredients:
- 1 ½ cups all-purpose flour
- 1 tsp baking powder
- 1 tsp ground cinnamon
- ½ tsp baking soda
- ½ tsp ground ginger
- ½ tsp ground allspice
- ¼ tsp salt
- ½ cup coconut oil, at room temperature
- ⅓ cup molasses
- ¼ cup white sugar
- 1 tsp vanilla extract

Directions:

1. Carefully preheat the oven to 350°F. Prepare two baking trays with parchment paper liners.
2. In a mixing bowl, combine the salt, cinnamon, ginger, allspice, baking soda, and baking powder.
3 .Add the vanilla extract to the coconut oi l, molasses, and sugar mixture. For about 2 minutes, or until a sticky dough forms, add the flour mixture. The dough should spend two hours in the refrigerator after being wrapped in plastic wrap.

4. On a floured surface, roll the dough into a 14- to 12-inch thickness. Lay out the cookies on the baking sheets after using a floured cookie cutter to make them.
5. Gently brown for 8 to 10 minutes in a preheated oven.

Nutritional Information: Calories 2050; Fat 111g; Sodium 1264mg; Carbs 252g; Fiber 7g; Sugar 104g; Protein 19.6g

Blueberry Muffins

Preparation time: 10 minutes

Cooking time: 35 minutes
Serves: 4
Ingredients:
cooking spray
- 2 cups fresh blueberries
- 2 cups all-purpose flour
- 1 cup lightly packed brown sugar
- ½ cup unsweetened applesauce
- ½ cup soy milk
- ¼ cup soy margarine
- 1 tbsp baking powder
- 1 tsp vanilla extract
- ½ tsp salt

Directions:
1. Carefully preheat the oven to 350°F. 12 mini muffin cups with paper liners or cooking spray on them
2. A mixing bowl should have the following ingredients: blueberries, flour, sugar, applesauce, soy milk, soy margarine, baking powder, vanilla extract, and salt. Half-full muffin tins should be used.
3. Bake for 35 minutes, or until the tops are crisp, in a preheated oven. Allow to cool slowly on a rack.

Nutritional Information: Calories 683; Fat 13g; Sodium 455mg; Carbs 137g; Fiber 4g; Sugar 84g; Protein 8g

Basil Oatmeal Patties

Preparation time: 10 minutes
Cooking time: 15 minutes
Serves: 5
Ingredients:
- 4 cups water
- 4 cups quick-cooking oats
- ½ onion, chopped
- ⅓ cup vegetable oil

- ½ cup spaghetti sauce
- ½ cup chopped pecans
- ¼ cup nutritional yeast
- 2 tsp garlic powder
- 1 tsp dried basil
- 2 tsp onion powder
- 1 tsp ground coriander
- 1 tsp sage
- 1 tsp active dry yeast

Directions:

1. Carefully preheat the oven to 350°F. Greasing a baking sheet is necessary.
2. Add the oatmeal to a pot of boiling water.
3. Lower the temperature to a low level and cover. Cook for 5 to 10 minutes, or until the oats are soft and the water has been absorbed.

4. After that, turn off the heat and let the oatmeal sit for 5 minutes.
5. Combine the oats with the onion, oil, spaghetti sauce, pecans, nutritional yeast, basil, coriander, onion powder, garlic powder, and active yeast. After thoroughly combining, shape into patties.
6. Arrange the patties evenly on the baking sheet that has been greased.
7. After 30 minutes of baking, turn the dish over once to the other side.
8. Dish out and savor!

Nutritional Information: Calories 317; Fat 23.6g; Sodium 442mg; Carbs 30g; Fiber 8g; Sugar 3g; Protein 11g

Orange Cake

Preparation time: 10 minutes
Cooking time: 30 minutes

Serves: 3

Ingredients:

- 1 large orange, peeled
- 1 ½ cups all-purpose flour
- 1 cup white sugar
- ½ cup vegetable oil
- 1 ½ tsp baking soda
- ¼ tsp salt

Directions:

1. Pre-heat the oven to 350 degrees Fahrenheit. A baking sheet has to be greased.

2. Pour boiling water into a saucepan and add the oatmeal. 3. Reduce the heat to a low setting and cover. Cook the oats for 5 to 10 minutes, or until tender and the water has been absorbed.
4. After that, remove the oatmeal from the heat and let it stand for five minutes.
5. Combine the nutritional yeast, basil, coriander, onion powder, oil, pecans, spaghetti sauce, and oats with the other ingredients. Create patties after completely mixing. 6. Evenly distribute the patties on the oiled baking sheet. 7. Bake for 30 minutes, then flip the dish over to the other side. 8. Serve up and enjoy!

Nutritional Information: Calories 692; Fat 36.7g; Sodium 817mg; Carbs 87g; Fiber 3g; Sugar 38g; Protein 7g

Herbed Mushroom Stuffing

Preparation time: 10 minutes
Cooking time: 1 hour 20 minutes
Serves: 5
Ingredients:

- 1 loaf of vegan, gluten-free, brown rice bread (such as Food for Life®), cubed
- 2 tbsp vegan margarine (such as Earth Balance®)
- 1 ½ cups mixed forest mushrooms, diced
- 1 ¼ cups sweet onion, chopped
- 2 ½ tsp dried sage
- 1 ½ tsp dried rosemary
- ½ tsp dried thyme
- sea salt, to taste
- freshly ground black pepper to taste
- 6 tbsp vegan margarine (such as Earth Balance®), melted
- 1 ½ cups low-sodium vegan broth
- 8 ounces fresh cranberries
- 1 cup chopped Granny Smith apple, peeled
- ⅓ cup minced fresh parsley

Directions:

1. Carefully preheat the oven to 350°F.
2. Use aluminum foil to line a baking tray.
3. Evenly distribute the bread pieces on the prepared baking sheet coated with foil. In a preheated oven, toast the bread for 10 minutes, or until fragrant and light brown.

4. Move the baking sheet to a cool place so it can cool. After that, place the cooled bread cubes in an appropriate mixing dish.
5. Melt 2 tbsp of margarine in a big pot over medium heat while the bread is toasting.
6. Add the onions and mushrooms. Cook the mixture for at least five minutes, or until the onions are just beginning to turn translucent. Add a little bit of vegetable broth if it needs more moisture, and season to taste with sage, rosemary, thyme, salt, and black pepper. For a further 2 minutes, stir with a wooden spoon to combine.
7. In a mixing bowl, combine the toasted bread and the mushroom mixture. Toss to distribute evenly.Add the cranberries, apple, and

parsley after combining the mixture with 6 tbsp of melted margarine and vegan broth. Blend gently but thoroughly.Aluminum foil should be placed over the filling in a casserole dish.

8. Bake in a preheated oven for 45 minutes; check after 25 minutes to avoid scorching. Gently stir after removing the lid.

9. Bake for approximately 15 minutes, or until the top is brown. Before serving, let it cool for a while.

Nutritional Information: Calories 373; Fat 20g; Sodium 131mg; Carbs 47g; Fiber 6g; Sugar 26g; Protein 6g

Lemony Artichokes

Preparation time: 15 minutes
Cooking time: 23 minutes
Serves: 3
Ingredients:

- 2 large artichokes
- 1 ½ cups water
- 2 teaspoons extra-virgin olive oil
- 1 lemon
- ⅛ tsp salt
- ⅛ teaspoon freshly ground black pepper

Directions:

1. Use a sharp knife to trim the ends of the artichoke so that the bases are flat.

2. Place the stainless steel trivet in the bottom of a 3- or 6-quart pressure cooker.

3. Pour 1 1/2 cups of water into the bowl to steam.

4. Place the artichokes on the trivet with their flat sides facing up. On the lid, knock

5. To set the cooking duration to 23 minutes at high pressure, use

the manual setting. Either the manual release or the natural release may be used.

6. To serve the artichokes, arrange them on a large plate using tongs.

7. Squeeze the lemon over the arms and sprinkle the olive oil on top. Sprinkle with salt and pepper, then serve right away.

Nutritional Information: Calories 86; Fat 0.3g; Sodium 311mg; Carbs 18.4g; Fiber 9g; Sugar 1.7g; Protein 6.6g

Simple Carrots

Preparation time: 10 minutes
Cooking time: 2 minutes
Serves: 8
Ingredients:
- 2 pounds fresh carrots, washed
- 1 cup water
- 1 teaspoon fresh or dried thyme, chopped
- 1 tbsp melted ghee, butter, or coconut oil

Directions:
1. Roughly chop the carrots into 1-inch cubes.
2. Fill the 6-quart pressure cooker's base with water. Add the rabbits.
3. Close the lid and check that the valve is set to seal. The cook time should be set at 2 minutes on high pressure.

4. When the cooking process is over, carefully quick-release the pressure.
5. Remove the cover and pour the water and vegetables into a casserole.
6. Pour the melted ghee or coconut oil over the drained carrots in a serving dish. Add the thyme, and serve warm or at room temperature.

Nutritional Information: Calories 52; Fat 0.7g; Sodium 79mg; Carbs 11.2g; Fiber 3.3g; Sugar 5.5g; Protein 1.3g

Vegan Cashew Macaroni and Cheese

Preparation time: 10 minutes
Cooking time: 45 minutes
Serves: 3
Ingredients:
- 1 (8 ounces) package uncooked elbow macaroni
- 1 tbsp vegetable oil
- 1 medium onion, chopped
- 1 cup cashews
- ⅓ cup lemon juice
- 1 ⅓ cups water
- salt to taste
- ⅓ cup canola oil
- 4 ounces roasted red peppers, drained
- 3 tbsp nutritional yeast
- 1 tsp garlic powder
- 1 tsp onion powder

Directions:

1. Carefully preheat the oven to 350°F.
2. Heat up a large pot of water that has been lightly seasoned.
3. Stir in the macaroni. Cook until al dente, which takes at least 8 to 10 minutes. then flush. Place in a medium baking dish.

4. Position a medium pot and set the temperature to medium-low. The vegetable oil is warmed.
5. Include an onion. Cook the onion until it is tender and lightly browned. Fold the macaroni in slowly.
6. Use a blender or food processor to incorporate cashews, lemon juice, water, and salt. Add the nutritional yeast, roasted red peppers,

canola oil, garlic powder, and onion powder gradually to the mixture. Blend until the mixture is flawless. Pasta and onions should be properly combined.

7. In a preheated oven, bake for 45 minutes, or until lightly browned. Before serving, let the food cool for 10 to 15 minutes.

Nutritional Information: Calories 814; Fat 53g; Sodium 1277mg; Carbs 66g; Fiber 5.6g; Sugar 11g; Protein 24g

Fried Jalapeno Cornbread

Preparation time: 10 minutes
Cooking time: 20 minutes
Serves: 2
Ingredients:
- 1 tbsp flaxseed meal
- 3 tbsp water
- cooking spray
- 1 cup stone-ground yellow cornmeal
- ⅔ cup all-purpose flour
- ¼ cup nutritional yeast
- 2 tbsp white sugar
- 2 ¼ tsp baking powder
- ½ tsp ground black pepper
- 1 tsp kosher salt
- ⅓ cup vegetable oil
- 1 cup unsweetened almond milk
- 1 large jalapeno pepper, seeded and minced

Directions:

1. Fill a small dish with water and add the flaxseed meal; stir to mix. After that, allot 10 minutes.
2. In the meantime, heat an air fryer to 350°F as directed by the manufacturer. Spray cooking spray into a 6-inch heat-resistant inner

pot.

3. In a medium mixing bowl, combine the nutritional yeast, sugar, cornmeal, flour, baking powder, salt, and pepper. Almond milk, oil, and the flaxseed-water mixture must all be well blended before being added. Add the jalapeo and pour the prepared pot into the air fryer.

4. Cook in a hot air fryer for 15 minutes. With tongs, remove the inner pot, turn the cornbread, and air fry for an additional five minutes, or until a toothpick inserted in the center comes out clean. Serve warm.

Nutritional Information: Calories 889; Fat 44g; Sodium 1290mg; Carbs 113g; Fiber 14g; Sugar 19g; Protein 21g

Salads and Sides Recipes

Mint Almond-Quinoa Tabbouleh

Preparation time: 10 minutes
Cooking time: 20 minutes
Serves: 2 to 3

Ingredients:

- 2 cups cooked quinoa
- 1 bunch mint, leaves picked
- 1 bunch flat-leaf parsley
- ½ small red onion, finely chopped
- ¼ cup lemon juice
- ¼ cup extra-virgin olive oil or avocado oil
- ½ cup whole almonds
- ½ cup chia or sunflower seeds
- 1 cup cherry tomatoes
- 1 avocado, optional
- 1 cup chopped kale or dandelion
- low-fat yogurt, to serve, optional

Directions:

1. Prepare the quinoa and let it cool. Chop off and discard the top half of the parsley stems. Mint, leaves, and the remaining bunch of parsley should all be coarsely chopped.
2. In a salad dish, mix the herbs and onion. Add the mixture to the drained quinoa.
3. Use olive oil and lemon juice to season everything well. Season the salad after combining the remaining ingredients.

Nutritional Information: Calories 619; Fat 43g; Sodium 50mg; Carbs 51g; Fiber 13g; Sugar 10g; Protein 14g

Lemony Greek Salad

Preparation time: 10 minutes
Cooking time: None
Serves: 4

Ingredients:

- 1 head iceberg lettuce
- 1 head romaine lettuce
- 1 pound plump tomatoes
- 6 ounces Greek or black olives, sliced
- 4 ounces sliced radishes
- 4 ounces low-fat feta or goat cheese
- 2 ounces anchovies (optional)

Dressing:

- 3 ounces olive oil or avocado oil
- 3 ounces fresh lemon juice
- 1 tsp dried oregano
- 1 tsp black pepper
- 1 tsp salt
- 4 cloves garlic, minced

Directions:

1. Lettuce needs to be cleaned before being cut into small pieces. Quartering tomatoes is recommended.
2. Combine the olives, lettuce, tomatoes, and radishes in a sizable mixing bowl. The dressing's components should be combined with the vegetables.
3. Half-fill a tiny serving bowl with the mixture. Top the crumbles of feta or goat cheese with anchovy fillets.

Nutritional Information: Calories 407; Fat 32g; Sodium 1607mg; Carbs 23g; Fiber 8.8g; Sugar 8g; Protein 12g

Lemony Cucumber Salad

Preparation time: 4 minutes plus 2 to 3 hours for refrigerating
Cooking time: None
Serves: 2 to 3

Ingredients:

- 2-3 cucumbers, sliced
- 2 tsp salt
- 3 tbsp lemon juice
- ¼ tsp paprika
- ¼ tsp white pepper
- ½ clove garlic, minced
- 4 fresh green onions, diced
- 1 cup thick Greek yogurt
- ¼ tsp paprika

Directions:

1. Cut cucumbers into thin slices, sprinkle with salt, and toss. Give yourself an hour to prepare.
2. Set aside a combination of white pepper, garlic, paprika, lemon juice, and water. Slices of cucumber should be squeezed dry one at a time, then placed in the bowl. Eliminate and discard the liquid.
3. In a mixing dish, combine the yogurt, green onions, and lemon juice. Combine everything, then sprinkle paprika or dill on top.

4. Chill for a couple of hours.

Nutritional Information: Calories 212; Fat 1g; Sodium 1617mg; Carbs 41g; Fiber 5.4g; Sugar 27g; Protein 12g

Radish and Tomato Salad

Preparation time: 8 minutes
Cooking time: None

Serves: 3 to 4

Ingredients:

- 1 medium head romaine lettuce, torn
- 3 small tomatoes, diced
- 1 medium cucumber, sliced
- 1 small green bell pepper, sliced
- 1 small onion, cut into rings
- 6 radishes, thinly sliced
- ½ cup flat-leaf parsley, chopped
- ⅓ cup olive oil or avocado oil
- 3 tbsp lemon juice
- 1 garlic clove, minced
- Salt & pepper
- 1 tsp fresh mint, minced

Directions:

1. Slice the cucumbers thinly, season with salt, and toss. Spend an hour getting ready.

2. Set aside a mixture of water, white pepper, garlic, paprika, and lemon juice. Cucumber slices should be squeezed dry one at a time before being added to the dish. Remove and throw away the liquid.

3. Combine the yogurt, green onions, and lemon juice in a mixing bowl. Mix everything together, then top with paprika or dill.
4. Wait a few hours before relaxing

Nutritional Information: Calories 110; Fat 6.8g; Sodium 178mg; Carbs 11.6g; Fiber 4.5g; Sugar 5.6g; Protein 3g

Lemony Tuna Tomato Salad

Preparation time: 8 minutes
Cooking time: None

Serves: 1
Ingredients:
- 1 can tuna in water, drained
- ⅓ cup four bean mix (or just white or red beans), drained, rinsed
- 1 tomato, deseeded, chopped
- 1 large celery stick, trimmed, finely chopped
- ½ small onion, halved, thinly sliced
- ½ cup flat-leaf parsley leaves, chopped
- ½ lemon, rind finely grated, juiced
- 1 garlic clove, crushed
- 1 tbsp extra-virgin olive oil

Directions:

1. Combine all ingredients, then plate.

Nutritional Information: Calories 399; Fat 17g; Sodium 661mg; Carbs 26g; Fiber 7.5g; Sugar 5.7g; Protein 39g

Mayo Pasta Salad

Preparation time: 15 minutes plus 2 hours for refrigerating
Cooking time: 15 minutes
Serves: 5
Ingredients:
- 1 (16 ounces) package dried rotini pasta
- 1 ½ cups medium chunky salsa
- 1 cup mayonnaise
- ½ cup sour cream
- 1 (16 ounces) can black beans, rinsed and drained
- 1 (11 ounces) can Mexican-style corn with red and green peppers, drained
- ½ cup chopped red bell pepper

- 2 green onions, sliced thin
- 1 (4.25-ounce) can slice black olives, drained
- ½ tsp garlic powder
- ½ tsp ground cumin, or to taste
- ½ tsp dried cilantro, or to taste
- 1 tsp salt
- ground black pepper to taste

Directions:

1. Boil some mildly salted water in a big pot, add the rotini, and cook for 8 minutes, or until the pasta is tender to the bite but still hard to the bite. Drain. Rinse thoroughly until completely cool under cold running water.

2. Toss the cold pasta with the mixture of the salsa, mayonnaise, sour cream, black beans, Mexican-style corn, red bell pepper, green onions, black olives, cumin, cilantro, salt, and pepper in a large mixing dish. Place the bowl in the refrigerator, wrapped in plastic, before serving.

Nutritional Information: Calories 920; Fat 23.6g; Sodium 1907mg; Carbs 151g; Fiber 30g; Sugar 8g; Protein 32g

Quinoa Cheese Salad

Preparation time: 8 minutes
Cooking time: None
Serves: 6
Ingredients:
For the salad
- 2 cups cooked quinoa
- 2-3 cups frozen green peas
- ½ cup low-fat feta cheese
- 6 ounces pork, cubed
- ½ cup freshly chopped basil and cilantro

- ½ cup almonds, pulsed in a food processor until crushed

For the dressing
- ⅓ cup lemon juice (1-2 large juicy lemons)
- ⅓ cup olive oil or avocado oil
- ¼ tsp salt (more to taste)
- a few tsp lucuma powder to taste

Directions:

1. Fill a pot with water, bring it to a boil, then turn down the heat.
2. Prepare the peas, covered, until they are a bright green color. Cook the pork in a skillet in the meantime.
3. In a mixing dish, combine the quinoa, pork, peas, feta, herbs, and almonds. Utilizing a food processor, puree each component of the dressing.

4. Combine the dressing with the salad's components. To taste, add salt and pepper to the food.
5. Place baby spinach on the side and serve.

Nutritional Information: Calories 268; Fat 12.8g; Sodium 352mg; Carbs 23.7g; Fiber 4.4g; Sugar 5g; Protein 14.7g

Grilled Asparagus-Spinach Salad

Preparation time: 8 minutes
Cooking time: 10 minutes
Serves: 1
Ingredients:
- ¼ cup olive oil
- ⅛ cup lemon juice
- 12 fresh asparagus spears
- 6 cups fresh spinach leaves
- ⅛ cup grated Parmesan cheese
- 1 tbsp seasoned slivered almonds

Directions:

1. Start a grill at a medium-low temperature. Lemon juice and olive oil should be combined in a dish. On the platter, twirl the asparagus to coat.

2. After 5 minutes of grilling, flip the asparagus once and brush with the olive oil mixture. Return the grilled chicken to the oil-covered plate after removing it from the grill.

3. In a sizing mixing bowl, combine the spinach, Parmesan cheese, and slivered almonds. Toss the asparagus with the salad's oil and lemon juice after cutting it into bite-sized pieces. After combining, serve.

Nutritional Information: Calories 596; Fat 59g; Sodium 379mg; Carbs 12.4g; Fiber 5g; Sugar 2.4g; Protein 10g

Broccoli-Crab Salad with Rotini

Preparation time: 4 minutes
Cooking time: 20 minutes
Serves: 3
Ingredients:

- 1 pound uncooked tri-color rotini pasta
- 1 tbsp extra-virgin olive oil
- 1 green bell pepper, seeded and diced
- 2 cups broccoli florets
- 1 cup diced carrots
- 8 ounces fresh crabmeat, well picked over
- 2 ounces sliced black olives, drained
- 3 tbsp minced sweet onion
- 1 cup mayonnaise
- 6 tbsp balsamic vinaigrette salad dressing
- 1 tsp of dried Italian herb seasoning
- ⅛ tsp ground black pepper, or to taste
- ¼ cup cherry tomatoes for garnish

Directions:

1. Cook the rotini for 8 minutes, or until cooked through but still firm to the bite, in a good saucepan with lightly salted water that has been heated to boiling. In a large mixing bowl, combine the drained pasta with extra virgin olive oil. While you prepare the other ingredients, place the food in the refrigerator for about 30 minutes.
2. In a mixing dish, combine the bell pepper, broccoli, carrots, crabmeat, olives, and onion. Combine spaghetti with
3. In a separate dish, combine the dressing ingredients—mayonnaise, balsamic vinaigrette, Italian seasoning, and black pepper—and whisk. Pour the dressing over the pasta salad. Blend everything together.

4. Top with cherry tomatoes, and serve chilled or at room temperature.

Nutritional Information: Calories 712; Fat 45.5g; Sodium 1475mg; Carbs 53.5g; Fiber 11g; Sugar 5g; Protein 24.6g

Tasty Celery Root Salad

Preparation time: 2 hours
Cooking time: 20 minutes
Serves: 1
Ingredients:
- 1 pound celery root
- 3 tbsp rapeseed oil
- 2 tbsp lemon juice
- 1 tbsp white wine vinegar
- salt to taste
- freshly ground black pepper to taste

Directions:

1. Trim the celery root into quarters after peeling. Put in a pot with lightly salted water.

2. After bringing the water to a boil, reduce the heat to low and simmer the potatoes for around 20 minutes. Drain and set aside to cool completely.Slice into pieces and place in a salad bowl.

3. In a small dish, mix the oil, lemon juice, vinegar, salt, and pepper. Celery root should be covered with the dressing. To enable tastes to meld, let the food marinate for at least two hours.

Nutritional Information: Calories 443; Fat 41.6g; Sodium 364mg; Carbs 15.6g; Fiber 7g; Sugar 6.8g; Protein 3g

Salmon-Shallot Pasta Salad

Preparation time: 4 minutes
Cooking time: 20 minutes
Serves: 2
Ingredients:
- ½ (16 ounces) package mezze (short) penne pasta
- 1 cup sliced and quartered cucumber
- 1 cup halved cherry tomatoes
- 2 tbsp minced shallot
- 1 (2.6 ounces) pouch of wild-caught pink salmon

Vinaigrette:
- ¼ cup extra-virgin olive oil
- 1 tbsp white wine vinegar
- 1 tbsp of freshly squeezed lemon juice
- 1 tsp lemon-pepper seasoning
- ½ tsp Dijon mustard
- ½ tsp salt
- ¼ tsp dried dill weed

Directions:

1. Get a large pot of mildly salted water warm. For about 10 minutes, boil the penne, stirring periodically, until it is tender but not mushy. Serve in a serving dish after draining and rinsing with cool water.
2. Arrange the cucumber, tomatoes, and shallots on top of the spaghetti. Broken-up salmon should be scattered on top.
3. To make the vinaigrette, whisk together the olive oil, vinegar, lemon juice, lemon-pepper seasoning, mustard, salt, and dill in a small mixing dish. Sprinkle the dressing over the salad and gently toss to combine.

Nutritional Information: Calories 470; Fat 31g; Sodium 763mg; Carbs 38g; Fiber 7g; Sugar 3.8g; Protein 12g

Tortellini and Veggies Salad

Preparation time: 4 minutes
Cooking time: 20 minutes
Serves: 2
Ingredients:
- 1 (9 ounces) package cheese tortellini
- 1 small red bell pepper, julienned
- ¾ cup broccoli florets, blanched
- ⅓ cup shredded carrots
- ⅓ cup pitted green olives
- 1 clove garlic, chopped
- ½ cup mayonnaise
- ¼ cup prepared basil pesto
- ¼ cup milk
- 2 tbsp grated Parmesan cheese
- 1 tbsp olive oil
- 1 tbsp distilled white vinegar
- 1 bunch fresh spinach leaves

Directions:

1. A large pot of moderately salted water should be heated. Tortellini should be cooked for 7 to 8 minutes, or until tender. Cool after draining

2. In a large mixing bowl, combine the cooked tortellini with the red bell pepper, broccoli, carrots, olives, and garlic.

3. Combine the mayonnaise, pesto, milk, Parmesan cheese, vinegar, and olive oil separately. Tortellini and vegetables should be coated with sauce. Refrigerate covered for an hour or until cold. Plate with spinach leaves on top .

Nutritional Information: Calories 751; Fat 38g; Sodium 1246mg; Carbs 75g; Fiber 8.6g; Sugar 6.5g; Protein 29g

Lemony Shrimp Salad with Pasta Shell

Preparation time: 10 minutes plus 2 to 3 hours
Cooking time: 15 minutes
Serves: 4
Ingredients:
- 1 ¼ cups mayonnaise, or more if needed
- 2 tsp Dijon mustard
- 2 tsp ketchup
- ¼ tsp Worcestershire sauce
- 1 tsp salt, or to taste
- 1 pinch of cayenne pepper, or to taste
- 1 lemon, juiced
- ⅓ cup chopped fresh dill

Salad:
- 1 (12 ounces) package small pasta shells
- 1 pound cooked, peeled, and deveined small shrimp, cut in half
- ½ cup finely diced red bell pepper
- ¾ cup diced celery
- salt and ground black pepper to taste

- 1 pinch of paprika for garnish
- 3 sprigs fresh dill, or as desired

Directions:

1. In a mixing dish, combine 1 1/4 cups mayonnaise, 134 cups chopped dill, 14 cups Dijon mustard, 14 cups ketchup, 14 cups Worcestershire sauce, salt, and cayenne pepper. Stir well until well combined. Refrigerate.

2. Boil salted water in a pot, add the pasta shells, and simmer for 8 to 10 minutes, or until tender. Pasta should be drained, then rinsed in cold water to give it a little chill. Place in a large mixing bowl.

3. Combine spaghetti and shrimp; add red bell pepper, celery, and dressing. After thoroughly combining, pour the dressing into the shells. Put the bowl in the fridge for two to three hours with plastic wrap on top.

4. Add extra salt, black pepper, lemon juice, and cayenne pepper to taste before serving. Add a little additional mayonnaise if the salad seems to be on the dry side. Add paprika and dill sprigs as a garnish.

Nutritional Information: Calories 453; Fat 26g; Sodium 1875mg; Carbs 32g; Fiber 6g; Sugar 3g; Protein 23g

Shrimp Salad with Cilantro Vinaigrette

Preparation time: 15 minutes
Cooking time: 20 minutes
Serves: 3

Ingredients:
- 1 tbsp olive oil
- 2 ¼ tsp smokehouse maple seasoning (such as McCormick® Grill Mates®)
- 1 ½ tsp lemon juice
- 12 ounces peeled and deveined shrimp

Cilantro Vinaigrette:
- ¼ cup extra-virgin olive oil
- 2 tbsp honey
- 2 tbsp fresh lime juice
- 2 tbsp chopped cilantro
- 1 tbsp balsamic vinegar
- salt and ground black pepper to taste

Salad:
- 4 cups mixed salad greens, or more to taste
- ½ cup thinly sliced English cucumber
- ⅓ cup freshly cooked corn
- ½ cup diced tomato
- ¼ cup sliced red onion
- 1 avocado, diced

Directions:

1. In a glass bowl, mix the olive oil, maple seasoning, and lemon juice. Add the shrimp and coat. Keep it chilled until you're ready to grill.
2. In a small mixing bowl, combine the olive oil, honey, lime juice, cilantro, balsamic vinegar, salt, and pepper. Set the vinaigrette aside.
3. Preheat either an indoor or outdoor medium-high grill.Serve the shrimp after threading them onto skewers. The shrimp should be grilled for approximately 2 minutes on each side, or until they are opaque and pink. Set the skewers aside after removing them.

4. Place mixed greens halfway up a big salad bowl. Sliced cucumber, corn, tomato, red onion, and avocado should be placed on top of the greens. Place the grilled shrimp in the center of the salad. Over the salad, drizzle the vinaigrette and toss to combine. Serve immediately.

Nutritional Information: Calories 443; Fat 24g; Sodium 1352mg; Carbs 32.7g; Fiber 8.8g; Sugar 19g; Protein 28g

Beans and Corn Salad

Preparation time: 4 minutes
Cooking time: None
Serves: 6

Ingredients:

- 1 (1 ounce) package of dry ranch dressing mix (such as Hidden Valley Ranch®)
- 1 cup buttermilk
- 1 cup fat-free plain yogurt
- ½ (1.25 ounce) package of taco seasoning mix, or more to taste

Salad:

- 8 cups torn romaine lettuce
- 2 roasted red peppers, diced
- 1 (14 ounces) can black beans, rinsed and drained
- 1 (14 ounces) can white corn, drained
- ¼ cup finely chopped sweet onion
- 1 (4 ounces) can dice green chile peppers
- 1 cup diced Roma tomatoes
- ½ cup shredded sharp Cheddar cheese
- 1 large avocado, peeled, pitted, and sliced
- ¼ cup chopped fresh cilantro (optional)

Directions:

1. In a bowl, combine the taco seasoning mix, buttermilk, yogurt, and dressing mix.
2. Place the lettuce in a large serving bowl.
3. In a mixing bowl, combine roasted peppers, black beans, corn, onion, and green chiles. On top of the lettuce, spread the mixture. Add tomatoes on top, then top with Cheddar cheese. Avocado slices should be arranged in a circle and overlapped. If desired, add cilantro as a garnish. Serving the dressing separately is appropriate.

Nutritional Information: Calories 465; Fat 12g; Sodium 598mg; Carbs 69.5g; Fiber 17g; Sugar 12.8g; Protein 25g

Sesame Almonds, Strawberry, and Spinach Salad

Preparation time: 8 minutes
Cooking time: None
Serves: 4 to 6

Ingredients:

- 2 tbsp black sesame seeds
- 1 tbsp poppy seeds
- ½ cup olive oil or avocado oil
- ¼ cup lemon juice
- ¼ tsp paprika
- 1 bag fresh spinach, chopped, washed, and dried
- 1-quart strawberries, sliced
- ¼ cup toasted slivered almonds

Directions:

1. Washing and chopping lettuce into tiny pieces is recommended. Quartering tomatoes is recommended.
2. Combine the olives, lettuce, tomatoes, and radishes in a large mixing bowl. The dressing's components should be combined with the veggies.
3. The mixture should be poured halfway into a small serving bowl.

4. If desired, top the feta or goat cheese crumbles with anchovy fillets.

Nutritional Information: Calories 274; Fat 25g; Sodium 49mg; Carbs 12.7g; Fiber 4.4g; Sugar 6g; Protein 3g

Curried Seven-Layer Salad

Preparation time: 1 hour
Cooking time: 15 minutes

Serves: 4

Ingredients:

- 2 cups small seashell pasta
- 4 carrots, peeled and julienned
- ½ head leaf lettuce, rinsed, dried, and chopped
- 1 medium cucumber, peeled, seeded, and diced
- ¾ cup frozen green peas
- ½ cup frozen whole-kernel corn
- 2 cups mayonnaise
- 2 tbsp brown sugar
- 1 tbsp curry powder
- ½ tsp garlic salt
- 1 cup shredded Cheddar cheese

Directions:

1. Heat some lightly salted water in a pot. Cook for 7 minutes or until the pasta is tender. Drain and rinse with cold water to cool.
2. Arrange the carrots in a single layer in the bottom of a large glass bowl, ideally one that has a virtually constant diameter throughout. The lettuce should be placed on top of the carrots. Over the lettuce, arrange the cucumber, peas, and corn in a layer. Distribute the spaghetti over the top when it has cooled and been drained.
3. In a separate small bowl, mix the mayonnaise, brown sugar, curry powder, and garlic salt. Shredded Cheddar cheese should then be evenly sprinkled over the pasta. Refrigerate for at least one hour, covered, before serving.

Nutritional Information: Calories 698; Fat 50.6g; Sodium 1276mg; Carbs 42g; Fiber 9.6g; Sugar 8.8g; Protein 20.5g

Beef Salad Topping

Preparation time: 8 minutes
Cooking time: 20 minutes

Serves: 2
Ingredients:
- ½ cup olive oil
- 1 tbsp soy sauce
- 1 onion, sliced
- 1 green bell pepper, seeded and thinly sliced
- 1 pound beef stew meat, cut into ½ inch pieces

Directions:

1. Heat the olive oil in a large pan over medium heat. In a mixing bowl, combine the soy sauce, onion, and green bell pepper. Cook the vegetables for 3 to 5 minutes, or until they are soft.
2. Add the stew meat made from beef. Cook for 15 minutes , stirring often, or until evenly browned.

Nutritional Information: Calories 813; Fat 64.6g; Sodium 309mg; Carbs 9.7g; Fiber 1.4g; Sugar 5g; Protein 51g

Rice and Peas Salad

Preparation time: 10 minutes
Cooking time: 15 minutes
Serves: 6
Ingredients:
- 2 cups water
- 1 cup white rice
- 6 eggs
- 1 (10 ounces) package of frozen peas, thawed
- 1 cup chopped celery
- ¼ cup chopped onion
- 1 (4 ounces) jar diced pimento
- 1 cup mayonnaise
- 1 tsp prepared mustard
- 1 tbsp lemon juice

- ¼ cup sweet pickle relish

Directions:

1. Heat water in a pot until it boils. Add rice by stirring. Cook for 20 minutes with the heat set to low and the lid on. removing the heat and letting it cool
2. Fill the water in a pot with eggs and cold water. After bringing the mixture to a boil, turn off the heat. Covered, let eggs sit in boiling water for 10 to 12 minutes. Remove from the boiling water and set aside to cool before peeling and cutting.
3. Frozen peas should be rinsed in cold water. After straining, put everything in a large mixing bowl. Add the celery, onions, pimiento, rice, eggs, and so on. Combine the tuna, dill, mayonnaise, mustard, lemon juice, relish, salt, and pepper in a different mixing dish. To combine, toss in the vegetable mixture. Covered, refrigerate for at least 4 hours. Toss again before serving. Before serving, chill.

Nutritional Information: Calories 412; Fat 19g; Sodium 1054mg; Carbs 36.7g; Fiber 3.7g; Sugar 4.6g; Protein 22g

Ranch-Barbecue Chicken Salad

Preparation time: 15 minutes
Cooking time: 10 minutes
Serves: 6

Ingredients:

- 2 skinless, boneless chicken breast halves
- 1 head red leaf lettuce, rinsed and torn
- 1 head green leaf lettuce, rinsed and torn
- 1 fresh tomato, chopped
- 1 bunch cilantro, chopped
- 1 (15.25-ounce) can whole kernel corn, drained
- 1 (15 ounces) can black beans, drained
- 1 (2.8-ounce) can French fried onions

- ½ cup Ranch dressing
- ½ cup barbeque sauce

Directions:

1. Turn the grill to high heat.
2. Lightly oil the grill grate. The chicken should be grilled for six minutes on each side or until the juices run clear. Slice after removing it from the flame and letting it cool.
3. In a sizing mixing bowl, combine the corn, black beans, tomato, cilantro, red and green leaf lettuce, and tomato. Serve with French-fried onions and chunks of grilled chicken.

4. In a small bowl, mix the ranch dressing and barbecue sauce. Mix the sauce with the salad to coat it, or serve it as a dipping sauce on the side.

Nutritional Information: Calories 503; Fat 12g; Sodium 676mg; Carbs 73g; Fiber 15.6g; Sugar 12.6g; Protein 29g

Chicken and Greens Salads

Preparation time: 4 minutes
Cooking time: 20 minutes
Serves: 5

Ingredients:

- 10 ounces cucumber ranch salad dressing
- 2 tbsp Buffalo-style hot pepper sauce (such as Frank's® RedHot)
- 4 stalks of celery, cut into ⅛-inch slices
- 4 medium carrots, cut into ⅛-inch slices
- 15 ounces cooked chicken, cut into bite-sized pieces
- 10 cups salad greens
- 1 ¼ cups crumbled blue cheese
- ¾ cup croutons (optional)

Directions:

1. Combine ranch dressing and spicy sauce in a small bowl. Divide the dressing into five quart-sized glass canning jars with wide mouths to create the first layer. Equal parts of carrots and celery should be used to create the following two layers:
2. Add 3 ounces of chicken to each container. In each jar, 2 cups of salad greens are layered on top of the chicken, followed by 1/4 cup blue cheese.Store the jars in the refrigerator until needed.
3. Five little covered containers should each contain an equal amount of croutons. When you're ready to eat, combine the jar's contents with the croutons in a bowl.

Nutritional Information: Calories 616; Fat 47g; Sodium 1Ingredients:mg; Carbs 15.3g; Fiber 4.2g; Sugar 5.8g; Protein 33.3g

Marinated Carrot and Celery Salad

Preparation time: 10 minutes plus 4 hours for refrigerating
Cooking time: 20 minutes
Serves: 4
Ingredients:
- 2 pounds carrots, sliced
- 1 (10.75 ounces) can condensed tomato soup
- ¼ cup white sugar
- ½ cup white vinegar
- ¼ cup canola oil
- 1 tsp prepared mustard
- 1 tsp Worcestershire sauce
- ½ cup chopped celery
- ½ cup chopped green onion
- 1 green bell pepper, seeded and cut into strips

Directions:

1. Boil a large pot of water, add the carrots, and cook for 3 to 5 minutes, or until soft. drain, then put aside.
2. In a sizable mixing bowl, combine the soup, sugar, vinegar, oil, mustard, and Worcestershire sauce. Add the pepper, onion, celery, and carrots and toss to coat. To give the carrots time to marinate, put them in the fridge for at least 4 hours.

Nutritional Information: Calories 270; Fat 17g; Sodium 286mg; Carbs 28.5g; Fiber 8.7g; Sugar 15g; Protein 3.5g

Dijon Red Leaf Salad

Preparation time: 10 minutes
Cooking time: None
Serves: 1
Ingredients:
  • 1 head red leaf lettuce
  • 1 red bell pepper, chopped
  • 1 stalk green onion, thinly sliced
Dressing:
  • 3 tbsp extra-virgin olive oil
  • 1 tbsp red wine vinegar
  • 1 tbsp balsamic vinegar
  • 1 tbsp lemon juice
  • ½ tsp salt, or to taste
  • ¼ tsp Dijon mustard, or more to taste
  • freshly ground black pepper to taste
Directions:

1. Use a salad spinner to clean and separate the red leaf lettuce leaves. Cut the leaves into bite-sized pieces, then put them in a salad bowl with the bell pepper and onions.
2. In a resealable container, combine the following ingredients: olive oil, red wine vinegar, balsamic vinegar, lemon juice, salt, mustard,

and pepper. Close the lid and shake to combine.

3. Dress the salad however much you want, then toss to combine. Any dressing that is left should be refrigerated.

Nutritional Information: Calories 455; Fat 41.6g; Sodium 1266mg; Carbs 16.8g; Fiber 4.3g; Sugar 7g; Protein 5.5g

Basil Fiesta Salad

Preparation time: 15 minutes
Cooking time: 30 minutes
Serves: 4
Ingredients:

- 2 lemons, juiced, divided
- 1 bunch of fresh basil leaves, divided
- 2 cloves garlic, crushed and peeled
- 2 tbsp olive oil, divided
- 1 tbsp shredded Parmesan cheese, or to taste
- salt and ground black pepper to taste
- ½ pound skinless, boneless chicken thighs
- 1 small onion, thinly sliced
- 2 tbsp vinegar
- 1 tbsp honey
- 1 (8 ounces) package kale, ribs removed and leaves torn into pieces
- 1 English cucumber, cubed
- 1 large heirloom tomato, cubed
- 1 large carrot, cubed
- 1 cup fresh corn kernels
- ½ (15 ounces) can black beans, rinsed and drained
- ½ (6 ounces) can black olives

Directions:

1. Carefully preheat the oven to 375°F.
2. Blend half a lemon's juice, half the basil, 1 tbsp of olive oil, Parmesan cheese, salt, and pepper in a food processor until smooth. The chicken thighs should be placed in a nonstick baking dish.
3. Roast chicken thighs in a preheated oven for 30 minutes. The chicken should be taken out of the oven and covered with the combined mixture.

4. Bake the chicken once again for 15 minutes, or until the juices run clear and the middle is no longer pink. Allow 10 minutes for cooling. Shred the chicken using two forks. Set aside.
5. Heat the remaining olive oil in a skillet over medium-low heat. About 10 minutes of cooking time is required to fully cook and brown the onion. In a mixing dish, combine the remaining basil, lemon juice, vinegar, and honey. The dressing must be fully heated in 5 minutes.
6. In a large mixing bowl, combine the chicken, kale, cucumber, tomato, carrot, corn, black beans, and olives.
7. Work the heated dressing into the salad and toss to evenly coat.

Nutritional Information: Calories 453; Fat 12.8g; Sodium 323mg; Carbs 59.7g; Fiber 14g; Sugar 12.4g; Protein 30g

Avocado-Cobb Salad

Preparation time: 4 minutes
Cooking time: 20 minutes
Serves: 5
Ingredients:
- 6 tbsp oil, plus more for grilling
- 3 tbsp red wine vinegar
- 1 tbsp Dijon mustard
- 1 tsp honey

- 1 clove garlic, minced
- Salt and pepper
- 1 large head green leaf lettuce halved (5 Cup yield)
- 2 ripe vine tomatoes halved
- 2 firm avocados
- 2 ears corn, whole and cleaned
- 1 package Grimm's Bacon and Cheddar Bavarian Smokies
- 4 hardboiled eggs, diced
- ½ cup Grimm's Medium Cheddar Cheese, grated
- Grimm's Cheese tortilla wraps, grilled.

Directions:

1. Fire up the grill. In a small bowl, combine 6 tbsp oil, red wine vinegar, Dijon, honey, and garlic. Add salt and pepper, then set aside.
2. Add two tbsp of oil, two pinches of salt, and some pepper to the lettuce halves. Toss the tomato halves in two tbsp of oil and season with salt and pepper. Keep the avocado seeds in their shells after removing the seeds. Oil, salt, and pepper are used to season the inside of the avocados. 2 tbsp of oil, salt, and pepper should be added to the corn.
3. Place the smokies and corn on the grill to cook and sear the outside. Next, sear the lettuce, tomatoes, and avocados' insides over high heat, leaving the outsides mostly uncooked. You just care about the scorched taste.

4. Remove every component from the grill. The tomato should be chopped, the corn should be taken from the cob, and the avocados should be sliced. Smokies should be cut into half moons. It's time to assemble everything at this point.
5. On a large platter, arrange the charred lettuce first, then a row of tomatoes, hard-boiled eggs, sliced smoked salmon, Cheddar, avocados, and corn. Serve with the red wine vinaigrette and grilled tortillas.

Nutritional Information: Calories 987; Fat 80g; Sodium 901mg; Carbs 41.5g; Fiber 12g; Sugar 9g; Protein 30g

Mayo Chicken Salad

Preparation time: 10 minutes
Cooking time: 15 minutes
Serves: 5

Ingredients:

- cooking spray
- 2 pounds skinless, boneless chicken breast halves
- 1 tsp kosher salt, divided
- ¾ tsp ground black pepper, divided
- ¾ tsp onion powder
- 1 cup mayonnaise, or more to taste
- ½ cup sour cream
- ¼ cup sweet relish
- 3 stalks of green onions (white and light green parts only), minced
- 2 tbsp chopped fresh parsley
- 1 tbsp Dijon mustard
- 1 tbsp lemon juice
- 1 tsp dried dill weed
- ½ cup finely chopped celery

Directions:

1. Carefully preheat the oven to 300°F. Spray some cooking spray in a baking dish.

2. Apply the same amounts of onion powder, pepper, and salt to the chicken. Cover tightly with foil and place in the prepared baking dish.

3. Bake for about 1 hour and 20 minutes, or until the chicken is

tender and the juices run clear. Do not overbake. An instant-read thermometer should register at least 165°F in the center.

4.As soon as it is cool enough to handle, remove it from the oven, cover it, and leave it for 15 minutes. Any remaining chicken broth should be kept.

5.Make the dressing while the chicken is cooling. Add 1 cup mayonnaise, 1 cup sour cream, relish, green onions, parsley, Dijon, lemon juice, dill, and the remaining salt and pepper to a large mixing bowl.

6.Large chunks of chicken should be placed in the food processor's bowl. Pulse the chicken 3–5 times to achieve the desired level of shreddedness.

7.In a bowl, place the chicken. Toss the celery with the dressing to coat. Add more mayonnaise or any unused broth if you want to add more moisture.

8.Cover and chill for at least two hours before serving. Mix all ingredients together thoroughly before serving.

Nutritional Information: Calories 429; Fat 22.7g; Sodium 1082mg; Carbs 9g; Fiber 1.3g; Sugar 4.6g; Protein 45g

Lunch Recipes

Sesame Flatbread Pizza

Preparation time: 25 minutes
Cooking time: 1 hour 10 minutes
Serves: 5

Ingredients:

- 2 tsp grapeseed oil
- 1 ½ cups flour
- 1 tsp onion powder:
- 2 tsp agave syrup
- 1 tsp oregano
- 2 tsp sesame seed
- 1 tsp sea salt

Directions:

1. Set the oven to 400°F.
2. In a large bowl, combine the aforementioned ingredients and add 12 cups of purified spring water. After that, gradually add water as you form the dough into balls. Apply a thin layer of grapeseed oil on the baking sheet. To successfully roll the dough onto the baking sheet, add flour to your hands.
3. Use a fork to poke holes in the top of the crust after brushing it with grapeseed oil. The crust should then bake for at least 10 minutes. While you are waiting for the crust to cook, go ahead and make the pizza sauce. Add onions, pizza sauce, pepperoni, mushrooms, and Brazil nut cheese after the crust has fully cooked. Afterward, bake your pizza for at least one hour. After that, serve and take pleasure.

Nutritional Information: Calories 169; Fat 2.8g; Sodium 469mg; Carbs 31.4g; Fiber 1.3g; Sugar 2.3g; Protein 4g

Mushroom-Tomato Pasta

Preparation time: 25 minutes
Cooking time: 1 hour
Serves: 4

Ingredients:

- 2 packs enoki mushrooms, about 400 grams total
- 8 round slices butternut squash, fresh
- 3 medium white onions, peeled, sliced
- 4 medium bell peppers, cored, sliced
- 2 cups cherry tomatoes
- 1 ½ tsp sea salt
- 4 tbsp coconut oil

Directions:

1.Cut the butternut squash into eight slices, peel them, and then remove the seeds. Take a large pot half full with water, place it over medium-high heat, bring it to a boil, and then add butternut squash.
2.Cook for 30 to 45 minutes, or until the potatoes are tender, then drain and mash with a fork.Add the onion, bell pepper, and mushrooms into the pot, and then let it simmer for 15–20 minutes until tender.
3. Season with salt, remove the pot from the heat, and let the mixture cool for 15 minutes.
4. Add coconut oil, wait until it melts, and then stir well.
5. Divide the pasta evenly among four plates, top with cherry tomatoes, and serve.

Nutritional Information: Calories 192; Fat 14g; Sodium 883mg; Carbs 16g; Fiber 4.6g; Sugar 5g; Protein 4.5g

Awesome Zucchini Hummus Wrap

Preparation time: 15 minutes
Cooking time: 10 minutes
Serves: 4

Ingredients:
- ½ medium red onion; peeled, sliced
- 2 medium plum tomatoes, sliced
- 2 cups romaine lettuce, chopped
- 2 large zucchinis
- ½ tsp sea salt
- ½ tsp cayenne pepper
- 2 tbsp grapeseed oil
- 4 spelt flour tortillas
- 8 tbsp hummus, homemade

Directions:

1. Slice the zucchinis after cleaning them and trimming their ends. Next, prepare a grill pan over medium heat while liberally greasing it with oil.

2. Slices of zucchini should be added to a medium bowl along with salt, cayenne pepper, and oil. Toss until evenly coated.

3. Spread the zucchini slices out on the hot grill pan; cook for 3 minutes or until they are golden brown; then flip them over and cook for an additional 2 minutes. Set aside until needed.

Heat the tortillas:

Place them on the grill pan, and then cook them for 1 minute on each side, or until the bread is hot and has grill marks.

Assemble the wraps:

Spread 2 tbsp of hummus on one side of each tortilla, top with one-fourth of the zucchini slices, one-half cup of lettuce, and one-fourth of the tomato slices, working on one wrap at a time. Repeat with the remaining tortillas, wrap securely, and serve.

Nutritional Information: Calories 278; Fat 12g; Sodium 703mg; Carbs 36.7g; Fiber 3g; Sugar 7g; Protein 5.8g

Herbed Grain Burgers

Preparation time: 10 minutes
Cooking time: 15 minutes
Serves: 2
Ingredients:
- ¼ cup bell peppers, finely diced
- 1 tsp oregano
- 1 tsp basil
- Sea salt and cayenne pepper
- ¼ onion, diced
- 1 ½ cups garbanzo bean flour
- 1 tsp dill
- 1 tbsp grapeseed oil
- 1 ½ cups cooked grains

Directions:

1. Place the onions and pepper in a pan with a tbsp of grapeseed oil and cook until soft.
2. Combine the other ingredients in a sizable bowl with the sautéed vegetables.
3. Create patties with your fingers and cook them for about 4 minutes on each side, or until they are crunchy.

Nutritional Information: Calories 833; Fat 19g; Sodium 49mg; Carbs 133g; Fiber 23g; Sugar 18g; Protein 38g

Mushroom-Pepper Tacos

Preparation time: 10 minutes
Cooking time: 12 minutes
Serves: 4
Ingredients:
- 4 large Portobello mushrooms
- 2 medium red bell peppers, cored, sliced

- 4 medium green bell peppers, cored, sliced
- 2 medium white onions, peeled, sliced
- ⅔ tsp onion powder
- ⅔ tsp habanero seasoning
- ⅔ tsp cayenne pepper
- 1 key lime, juiced
- 2 tbsp grapeseed oil
- 2 medium avocados, peeled, pitted, sliced
- 8 tortillas, corn-free

Directions:
Prepare the mushrooms:

1. Mushrooms should have their stems and gills removed. After a thorough rinse, cut them into pieces that are 13 inches thick.
2. In a large skillet, heat 1 tbsp of the oil over medium heat. When the oil is hot, add the onion and bell pepper and cook for 2 minutes, or until the vegetables are tender-crisp.
3.Add the sliced mushrooms, season with all the seasoning, stir to combine, and cook for an additional 7–8 minutes, or until the vegetables are tender. Warm up the tortillas while you wait.

Assemble the tacos
Place a cooked fajita in the middle of each tortilla, top with avocado, and squeeze lime juice over everything. Serve immediately.

Nutritional Information: Calories 375; Fat 23g; Sodium 70mg; Carbs 41g; Fiber 12g; Sugar 6.8g; Protein 7g

Peppered Kale

Preparation time: 5 minutes
Cooking time: 15 minutes
Serves: 4
Ingredients:

- ¼ cup white onion, diced
- 1 bunch of kale, fresh
- ¼ cup red pepper, diced
- ¼ tsp sea salt
- 1 tsp crushed red pepper
- 2 tbsp grapeseed oil

Directions:

Prepare the kale:

1. Remove the stem, give it a thorough rinse, and then chop the leaves into bite-sized pieces.
2. Utilizing a salad spinner, drain well.
3. Take a sizable skillet, heat it over high heat, add the oil, add the onion and red pepper, season with salt, and cook for three minutes, or until the vegetables are starting to become tender.
4. Turn down the heat, add the kale leaves, toss to combine, then cover the skillet with a lid and simmer for an additional five minutes.
5. Return the lid to the pan, sprinkle red pepper over the kale, toss to combine, and cook for an additional 3 minutes or until the vegetables are tender. Serve immediately.

Nutritional Information: Calories 74; Fat 7g; Sodium 153mg; Carbs 2.7g; Fiber 0.9g; Sugar 1g; Protein 1g

Stir-Fried Tofu and Green Beans

Preparation time: 10 minutes
Cooking time: 5 minutes
Serves: 4

Ingredients:

- 1 pound firm tofu
- 3 medium-sized zucchinis
- 3 pieces tomatoes

- 1 piece red bell pepper
- 1 piece green bell pepper
- ½ pound green beans
- 1 to 1 ½ cup fresh coconut milk
- 2 tbsp cold-pressed extra-virgin olive oil
- sea salt as needed
- pepper as needed
- ½ tbsp curry powder
- ¼ tbsp of ginger
- fresh assorted selection of herbs

Directions:

1. Slice the tofu. Cut your zucchini into pieces. Cut the beans, tomatoes, and bell peppers into tiny pieces.
2. Take a pan, pour oil into it, and heat it over medium heat. Add the tofu and cook it for two to three minutes. Stir-fry the zucchini, beans, and bell pepper for two to three minutes. Cook for a bit after adding the tomatoes and coconut milk.
3. Add some herbs, ginger, salt, and pepper to the dish. Serve with some soba noodles or wild rice.

Nutritional Information: Calories 402; Fat 31g; Sodium 35mg; Carbs 17g; Fiber 6.7g; Sugar 6g; Protein 21.5g

Zoodles with Avocado Sauce

Preparation time: 10 minutes
Cooking time: 20 minutes
Serves: 4
Ingredients:
- 4 large zucchinis, destemmed
- 4 avocados; pitted, peeled, sliced
- 4 cups basil leaves
- 48 cherry tomatoes, sliced

- 1 ½ tsp salt
- 1 cup walnuts, chopped
- 8 tbsp key lime juice
- 1 cup water

Directions:

1. To prepare zucchini, cut off the ends of each one, then use a spiralizer or vegetable peeler to create noodles. Set aside until needed.
2. Add the avocado, basil, salt, and nuts to a blender. Add the lime juice and water and blend on high for 1–2 minutes, or until a smooth sauce forms.
3. Place the zucchini noodles in a large bowl, add the sauce that has been well incorporated, add the tomatoes, and toss until the noodles are evenly covered. Serve immediately.

Nutritional Information: Calories 500; Fat 43g; Sodium 899mg; Carbs 31g; Fiber 17.6g; Sugar 7.7g; Protein 9g

Tuna Bites with Walnuts

Preparation time: 15 minutes
Cooking time: None
Serves: 4

Ingredients:
- ⅔ sheet nori
- 2 cups walnuts, chopped
- 4 key limes, juiced
- 2 Roma tomatoes
- ¼ tsp onion powder
- ¼ tsp dried oregano
- ¼ tsp ginger powder
- ¼ tsp dried thyme
- ¼ tsp sea salt

- ¼ tsp cayenne powder
- 2 tbsp coconut oil

Directions:
Prepare the nori sheets:

1. To remove one-third of the nori sheet, fold it into three equal folds and cut along the first crease.
2. Now place the pieces of the cut third of the nori sheet on top of one another, fold them in half, and cut along the crease.
3. Carry out step 3 with the remaining nori sheet, then add the bits to the food processor.

Prepare the tomatoes:

1. Remove the tops, then divide each one into five equal pieces. Then, cover the food processor with the lid, add the remaining ingredients, and pulse for 3–4 minutes, until everything is well combined and blended.
2. Create rough balls out of the mixture, place them on a platter, and then serve.

Nutritional Information: Calories 344; Fat 33g; Sodium 150mg; Carbs 12g; Fiber 3.7g; Sugar 3.4g; Protein 6.9g

Curried Eggplant with Quinoa

Preparation time: 5 minutes
Cooking time: 5 minutes
Serves: 3
Ingredients:
- 1 piece roasted eggplant
- juice of 1 lemon
- 1 tsp sea salt
- 1 tsp curry powder

- Water as required
- Cooked quinoa required for serving

Directions:

1. Take out everything inside the eggplant shell.
2. In a food processor, combine the eggplant, lemon juice, sesame oil, salt, and curry powder. Process the mixture until smooth. Preheat a small saucepan over medium heat.
3. Put your saucepan with the eggplant mixture in it and gently reheat it for about five minutes. If necessary, thin it with water. The quinoa is delicious over the curried eggplants!

Nutritional Information: Calories 77; Fat 0.7g; Sodium 1169mg; Carbs 18g; Fiber 8.8g; Sugar 10g; Protein 3g

Marinated Portobello Burgers

Preparation time: 4 minutes
Cooking time: 20 minutes
Serves: 4

Ingredients:
- 4 large Portobello mushroom caps
- 2 large avocados; pitted, peeled, flesh sliced
- 2 medium tomatoes, sliced
- 2 cups purslane

Marinade：
- 2 tsp cayenne pepper
- 4 tsp dried basil
- 2 tsp dried oregano
- 1 tsp onion powder
- 6 tbsp olive oil

Directions:
Prepare the mushrooms:

Remove the stem from each mushroom before slicing off 12 inch of the top to slice them like a bun.

Prepare the marinade:

1. Place all the ingredients in a small bowl and whisk to thoroughly incorporate.
2. Place the prepared mushroom caps on a cookie sheet that has been lined with foil and greased with oil. Each mushroom cap should be filled with the marinade that has been prepared. After 10 minutes, let it rest.
3. In the meantime, preheat the oven to 425 degrees. The mushroom caps should be baked for another 10 minutes, 10 on each side, until they are tender.

4. To serve, place the stuffed baked mushroom caps cap-side up on plates and evenly distribute the avocado, tomato, and purslane inside. Serve immediately.

Nutritional Information: Calories 364; Fat 35.4g; Sodium 22mg; Carbs 13.5g; Fiber 8g; Sugar 2.5g; Protein 3.5g

Apple and Celery with Almonds

Preparation time: 60 minutes
Cooking time: None
Serves: 2
Ingredients:

- 10 ounces sliced up knob celery
- 6-7 ounces cubed up apples
- 2 or 3 cups water
- ⅓ cup almonds
- ½ lemon
- ½ tbsp salt
- Pepper as needed

Directions:

1. Place the apples, celery, and lemon juice in a medium bowl. Mix everything thoroughly. To make an exceptionally nice and smooth paste, pulse your almonds in a blender with a little water.
2. Put the paste in a bowl and add salt and pepper to taste. Blend thoroughly and set aside for 60 minutes.
3. Stir the paste into the bowl of apples before serving.

Nutritional Information: Calories 83; Fat 0.6g; Sodium 1865mg; Carbs 20g; Fiber 5g; Sugar 13g; Protein 1.7g

Potato, Parsley, and Pumpkin Patties

Preparation time: 10 minutes
Cooking time: 5 minutes
Serves: 2
Ingredients:
- 1 pound pumpkin
- 1 pound potatoes
- 2 ½ ounces soy flour
- 4 tbsp water
- 3 tbsp chopped up parsley
- sea salt as needed
- organic salt as needed
- a pinch of pepper
- cold pressed extra-virgin olive oil

Directions:

1. Peel the skins off of your potatoes and pumpkin. Both of them should be grated into large pieces using a grater.
2. 2 tbsp of soy flour and 4 tbsp of water should be placed in a bowl.
3. Grated pumpkin and potatoes should be placed in a separate

basin with soy flour. Flour the mixture, then thoroughly combine it. Add some pepper, parsley, and salt to taste.

4. Take a pan and heat it to a moderate temperature. Heat it up and add oil. Make patties from the mixture and cook them for a couple of minutes in hot oil until they are browned.

Nutritional Information: Calories 399; Fat 7.8g; Sodium 26mg; Carbs 69g; Fiber 10g; Sugar 12g; Protein 19.7g

Rosemary Salmon

Preparation time: 8 minutes
Cooking time: 15 minutes
Serves: 3
Ingredients:
- 2 wild caught sockeye salmon filets, 10 ounces total
- 1 tsp salt
- 2 tablespoons ghee
- 1 tbsp minced garlic, about 2-3 cloves
- 1 tablespoon chopped fresh rosemary
- zest of 1 orange
- juice of 2 oranges, about ⅓ cup
- 1 teaspoon tapioca starch

Directions:

1. As soon as the oven reaches 425°F, line a baking sheet with parchment paper.
2. Each filet should be salted with 1/2 tsp salt and baked for 6 to 8 minutes.
3. While the salmon bakes, combine the butter and garlic in a sauce pan and heat over medium heat for about three minutes.

4. Add the rosemary, orange zest, and orange juice. Cook for a further three minutes.
5. Tapioca starch should be well mixed in so that there are no lumps left. Turn off the heat after stirring until it has just slightly thickened.
6. Remove the savoy from the oven, top with the garlic orange sauce, and serve.

Nutritional Information: Calories 146; Fat 7g; Sodium 890mg; Carbs 4.8g; Fiber 0.6g; Sugar 1.8g; Protein 15g

Shrimp and Zoodles

Preparation time: 4 minutes
Cooking time: 20 minutes
Serves: 3 to 4
Ingredients:
- 3 cloves garlic, crushed
- 3 tbsp olive oil or avocado oil divided
- 1 pound raw shrimp peeled deveined
- Juice of 1 lemon
- 1 tsp lemon zest
- ¼ cup chicken broth
- 3 tbsp ghee
- 3 tbsp fresh chopped parsley
- Salt and pepper to taste
- 2 large zucchini

Directions:

1. To begin, combine 1 tbsp oil and 1 garlic clove.The shrimp should be coated and marinated for 30 minutes. (Optional, but it increases the shrimp's flavor.)
2. Heat the last 2 tbsp. a big sauce pan with oil. The shrimp won't be completely cooked after being added and cooking for 1-2 minutes on each side. Keep the oil in the pan and set it aside. Maintain the heat

in the pan.

3. Add the last of the garlic now and cook it for one minute, or until fragrant. Lemon juice, chicken broth, and zest are added. Cook for a further three minutes to reduce the sauce.

4. Add butter to the pan. Cook for a further three minutes, or until the sauce starts to thicken.

5. Return the shrimp to the pan and cook for 2 minutes on each side, covered with the sauce.

6.Spiralize your zucchini before preparing the zucchini noodles. Add about 1 tbsp of oil, then either bake at 375 degrees for 10 minutes or sauté for 5 minutes. You may also serve raw food.

7. To shrimp and zucchini sauce. To serve, garnish with fresh parsley.

Nutritional Information: Calories 319; Fat 21g; Sodium 1062mg; Carbs 8g; Fiber 2g; Sugar 5g; Protein 26g

Fried Rice with Veggies

Preparation time: 20 minutes
Cooking time: 60 minutes
Serves: 2
Ingredients:

- ½ cup sliced zucchini
- 1 tbsp grapeseed oil
- ½ cup sliced mushrooms
- ¼ cubed onions
- ½ cup sliced bell pepper
- 1 cup cooked quinoa
- cayenne pepper and sea salt to your taste

Directions:

1. Sauté the onion until it is properly fried in a pan with hot grapeseed oil. Place the vegetables in and give them at least 6 minutes to cool. Make sure the vegetables don't cook too long or get mushy.
2. 1 cup of cooked quinoa or wild rice should be added next. Cook until a light brown color appears. After that, serve and take pleasure.

Nutritional Information: Calories 202; Fat 8.8g; Sodium 13mg; Carbs 26.7g; Fiber 3.7g; Sugar 5g; Protein 5.7g

Crusted Salmon and Asparagus with Almonds

Preparation time: 8 minutes
Cooking time: 15 minutes
Serves: 4
Ingredients:
Almond herb mixture:
- ¼ cup ground almonds
- 1 tbsp fresh basil chopped, or dried
- 1 tbsp fresh parsley chopped, or dried
- 1 teaspoon fresh oregano, or dried
- salt & pepper to taste

Salmon & asparagus:
- ½ pound asparagus stalks
- 2 tbsp extra-virgin olive oil
- zest & juice from ½ lemon
- 4 6-ounce salmon fillets

Directions:

1. Preheat the oven to 400°F.
2. Combine the ground almonds, herbs, salt, and pepper in a small bowl. Set aside for the time being
3.Spread the asparagus on a baking sheet and sprinkle the salt with oil. Season the asparagus with a pinch of sea salt and half of the

lemon zest. toss to combine. To create room for the salmon, push the asparagus to the edges of the baking tray.

4. Lay the salmon fillets over the tray with the skin side down. Spoon the mixture of almonds and herbs evenly over the salmon pieces after squeezing the lemon juice over them. Add the remaining lemon zest and juice on top.
5. Roast the fish for 10 to 12 minutes at 400°F, or until it is well cooked.

Nutritional Information: Calories 659; Fat 11g; Sodium 10mg; Carbs 66g; Fiber 1.7g; Sugar 3.4g; Protein 85g

Spicy Shrimp Stir Fry

Preparation time: 15 minutes
Cooking time: 30 minutes
Serves: 5
Ingredients:
Spicy Aioli:
- ½ cup homemade mayo or purchased paleo mayo
- 1 clove garlic, minced
- 1 tsp sesame oil
- 1 ½ tsp lime juice or lemon juice
- 2 to 3 tsp hot sauce 30-day-whole-food – compliant
- Pinch cayenne pepper or to taste

Shrimp Stir Fry:
- 1 pound shrimp peeled
- 2 tbsp coconut oil
- Sea salt and pepper for shrimp*
- 6 cups slaw mix or a combination of shredded cabbage, carrots, brussels sprouts, etc.
- 3 tbsp coconut aminos
- 2 tbsp sesame oil

- 1 tsp hot sauce 30-day-whole-food compliant, optional
- 1 bunch scallions thinly sliced white or light green and green parts separated
- 3 cloves garlic minced
- 2 tsp ginger fresh, about 1" peeled and grated or minced

To prepare the Aioli:

Mayo, garlic, sesame oil, lime or lemon juice, hot sauce, and cayenne, if using, should be combined and whisked until smooth. Keep refrigerated until ready to use.

Stir Fry the Shrimp and Veggies:

1. Prepare all ingredients and have them ready to go before starting to cook since it won't take long.
2 .A1 tbsp coconut oil in a large nonstick skillet or wok over high heatIf desired, season the shrimp with salt, pepper, and a dash of cayenne pepper.
3. Add the shrimp in a single layer once the skillet is hot and ready to cook. Cook for approximately 2 minutes, turning once or twice, or until opaque. Cover and set aside while you prepare the vegetables.

4. Add the second tbsp of coconut oil and reduce the heat to medium. When the slaw or shredded vegetables start to soften, add them along with the white pepper, ginger, and garlic. Cook and stir for approximately a minute.
5. Cook for an additional minute or two, then add the coconut aminos, sesame oil, and spicy sauce (if using) to the skillet and toss. Lower the heat, add the shrimp back in, and stir to thoroughly blend. Remove from the heat and top with green onion.
6. Serve in bowls with a spicy aioli drizzle. Enjoy!

Nutritional Information: Calories 406; Fat 21.7g; Sodium 762mg; Carbs 42g; Fiber 4.3g; Sugar 9.6g; Protein 13.6g

Thai Seafood Soup

Preparation time: 20 minutes
Cooking time: 40 minutes
Serves: 8

Ingredients:

- 2 tbsp fat (ghee, olive oil)
- 4 cups bone broth (any kind you like)
- 3 tbsp cashew butter (or 1 cup cashew creamer or sup coconut cream for AIP)
- 3 pounds white fish filet (no scales or bones)
- 2 bay leaves
- 1 large Vidalia onion
- 2 inch nub of ginger
- 4 garlic cloves
- 3 carrots
- 2 tsp salt
- 4 baby bok choy
- 2 cans water chestnuts
- 3 lemons

To taste:

- 2 tbsp fish sauce, as you like to taste
- 1 bunch cilantro
- 2 tbsp wasabi powder

Directions:

1. Heat two tbsp of fat over medium heat in a large stockpot.
2. Slice the garlic, ginger, onions, and carrots finely.
3. Once the pot is heated, add the diced vegetables and bay leaf.

4. Cook, sometimes stirring, for about 8 minutes or until tender.
5. As you wait, cut your fish into 1-inch pieces, then chop, wash, and take apart your bok choy.
6. Peel off a few "triples" of lemon rind and add them to the saucepan.

7. When all the fish is cooked, add it to the pot and mix it well.
8. Add the salt, the cashew cream, the fish sauce, and the wasabi powder. Mix thoroughly.
9. Add the broth, bring to a boil, and then simmer for ten minutes.
10. Add the water chestnuts and bok choy. Stir. Bring on the summertime!
11 .Juice all of your lemons. Place aside.
12. Give the soup another 10 minutes to simmer.
13. Slice up your currency.
14. Include the lemon juice. Stir. Taste and adjust the salt as needed. Add some water if you want it to be thinner.
15. Serve generously with fresh cilantro!

Nutritional Information: Calories 532; Fat 27g; Sodium 2431mg; Carbs 30.4g; Fiber 6.4g; Sugar 9g; Protein 45g

Grilled Chicken Cobb Salad

Preparation time: 4 minutes
Cooking time: 20 minutes
Serves: 6

Ingredients:
- 4 bacon pieces, diced
- 2 boneless, skinless chicken breasts, thinly sliced
- 3 tbsp barbecue sauce, or more to taste
- 2 hefty eggs
- 6 cups romaine lettuce, chopped
- 2 diced Roma tomatoes
- 1 halved, seeded, peeled, and diced avocado
- 1 cup drained canned corn kernels
- 1 cup drained and rinsed canned black beans

Dressing for the buttermilk ranch:
- 1 tbsp buttermilk

- ¼ cup unsweetened Greek yogurt
- 1 tbsp sour cream
- ½ tsp dill, dried
- ½ tsp parsley, dry
- ¼ tsp powdered garlic
- Freshly ground black pepper, to taste
- Salt and pepper, to taste

Directions:

1. Combine buttermilk, Greek yogurt, sour cream, parsley, dill, garlic powder, salt, and pepper in a small bowl.
2. In a big skillet over medium heat, pour the oil. Cook for 6 to 8 minutes, or until the bacon is brown and crispy. Then, move it to a dish that has been lined with paper towels and set it aside.
3. Add salt and pepper to taste and season the chicken breasts. Cook, turning once, for about 3–4 minutes on each side, or until well done. Slice it into bite-sized pieces when it has fully cooled.

4. Combine the chicken and BBQ sauce in a medium bowl by gently mixing the ingredients.
5. Put the eggs in a big pot and pour 1 inch of cold water over them. Bring to a boil, then simmer for one minute on low heat. Eggs should be taken off the heat, covered with a tight-fitting lid, and left for 8 to 10 minutes. Before peeling and dicing, properly drain the vegetables and let them cool.
6. To make the salad, layer rows of bacon, BBQ chicken, eggs, tomatoes, avocado, corn, and beans on top of romaine lettuce in a big bowl.
7. Add a buttermilk ranch dressing garnish and serve right away.

Nutritional Information: Calories 285; Fat 10.7g; Sodium 218mg; Carbs 23.3g; Fiber 7g; Sugar 6g; Protein 26g

Dinner Recipes

Tahini Chicken Shawarma

Preparation time: 4 minutes
Cooking time: 4 minutes
Serves: 3

Ingredients:

- 1 cup cucumbers, shredded
- ¼ cup nonfat Greek yogurt, either the strained or the plain variety
- 1 tbsp tahini
- 2 tbsp lemon juice
- ½ tsp salt, divided
- 1 tbsp and 1 level tsp garlic powder
- 1 tsp, weighed and level, curry powder
- freshly ground black pepper, to taste
- 1 pound chicken breasts, boneless and skinless without excess fat or gristle
- 1 tbsp coconut oil
- large romaine lettuce leaves

Directions:

1. Increase the grill's heat setting to medium.
2. In a medium bowl, combine the diced cucumber, yogurt, tahini, lemon juice, and 1/4 tsp salt. Place aside.
3. Add the remaining 1/4 tsp of salt, the pepper, the curry powder, and the garlic powder to a second medium bowl. The chicken breasts should be sliced lengthwise into quarter-inch-wide strips before being added to the spice mixture to coat them. Combine the ingredients with 1 tbsp of oil by tossing them together.

4. Place the chicken on the grill and cook it, flipping it once, for about 2 minutes on each side. Do this repeatedly until the chicken is

cooked through.

5. To serve the meal, start by smearing a large lettuce leaf with a quarter cup of the cucumber-yogurt sauce. After that, scatter a fourth of the chicken over the sauce. Eat it by rolling it up like a taco!

Nutritional Information: Calories 404; Fat 15g; Sodium 723mg; Carbs 10.6g; Fiber 2.4g; Sugar 2.6g; Protein 56g

Shrimp-Stuffed Tomatoes with Spinach

Preparation time: 10 minutes
Cooking time: None
Serves: 3
Ingredients:
- ⅔ pound shrimp, cooked
- 3 tbsp plain, fat-free Greek yogurt.
- 1 tsp dried dill
- 3 medium tomatoes
- the black pepper and the salt (to taste)
- 1 cup spinach, roughly chopped

Directions:

1. Blend the spinach, shrimp, yogurt, spices, and other ingredients in a blender until smooth.
2. Remove the tomato's center pulp with a spoon.
3. Fill the tomatoes with the shrimp mixture and, if you'd like, season them with salt before serving.

Nutritional Information: Calories 136; Fat 1.2g; Sodium 134mg; Carbs 6.5g; Fiber 1.8g; Sugar 4g; Protein 26g

Balsamic Salmon Steaks

Preparation time: 10 minutes plus 4 to 6 hours for marinating

Cooking time: 20 minutes
Serves: 3
Ingredients:

- 6 5-ounce salmon or tilapia fillets, cut into fillets.
- 4 tbsp diluted fermented soy sauce
- 4 tbsp balsamic vinegar
- 4 tbsp thinly sliced green onions
- 4 stevia packets in total
- 4 whole garlic cloves, minced
- 1 ½ tsp ginger powder
- ½ pinch dried crushed red pepper flakes
- 1 tsp sesame oil
- ½ tsp salt

Directions:

1. Arrange the salmon fillets in a non-permeable glass dish that is about the midpoint in size.
2. Combine the toasted sesame oil, soy sauce, vinegar, green onions, garlic, ginger, and crushed red pepper flakes in another dish of the same size. Garnish with more green onions.
3. Whisk all of the ingredients together before pouring them over the fish. Make sure to cover and keep the salmon cold while marinating it for 4 to 6 hours in the fridge.

4. To prepare an outside grill, move the coals to a spot about 5 inches away from the grate. Next, drizzle a thin coating of oil over the grate.
5. Position the fillets on a grill five inches from the embers and cook them for 10 minutes per inch of thickness, measured at the thickest section of the fillet, or until the fish easily breaks apart when tested with a fork. You should turn the meat over halfway through the cooking process.

Nutritional Information: Calories 544; Fat 26g; Sodium 1944mg; Carbs 12.8g; Fiber 0.8g; Sugar 9g; Protein 60.6g

Avocado Tuna Cucumber Roll

Preparation time: 8 minutes
Cooking time: None
Serves: 1
Ingredients:

- ¼ cucumber
- 1 can tuna
- ½ avocado
- 2 tsp mustard in the yellow color (yellow or Dijon)
- salt and pepper (to taste)

Directions:
1. Combine tuna, avocado, and mustard in a bowl.
2. Slice the cucumber into pieces that are one-fiftieth of an inch thick.
3. Before discarding the cucumber slices, take the slices and remove the seeds.
4. Make sure to completely fill the centers of the cucumbers with the tuna mixture.
5. Season with salt and pepper and savor!
Nutritional Information: Calories 334; Fat 17g; Sodium 700mg; Carbs 14.7g; Fiber 8g; Sugar 4.6g; Protein 35g

Italian Instant Pot Fish

Preparation time: 10 minutes
Cooking time: 15 minutes
Serves: 4
Ingredients:

- ¼ cup water

- 4 frozen white fish fillets, about 3-4 ounce each
- 12 cherry tomatoes
- 12-14 black olives
- 2 tablespoons marinated baby capers
- ⅓ cup sliced roasted red peppers
- 2 tablespoons olive oil
- ½ teaspoon salt
- A pinch of chili flakes
- Garnish: chopped fresh parsley or basil (optional)

Directions:

1. Water should be added to the Instant Pot.

2. Frozen fish fillets should be added to the water. The remaining ingredients should be added (spread out around and on top). Sprinkle with sea salt and chili flakes and drizzle with olive oil.

3.Shut the lid. Set the pressure cooker to manual or high pressure for 4 minutes. The Instant Pot will begin to build pressure and begin cooking after three beeps. Allow the pressure to naturally release for 7 to 8 minutes after the timer sounds before performing the quick release to let the steam out.

4. Open the lid and carefully remove the fish fillets using a spatula. Place the cooked ingredients on top of the broth, then serve. Add a little chopped parsley or basil as a garnish.

Nutritional Information: Calories 1099; Fat 76g; Sodium 2922mg; Carbs 15g; Fiber 6g; Sugar 8.5g; Protein 87.5g

Fried Mahi Mahi Bites

Preparation time: 10 minutes
Cooking time: 15 minutes
Serves: 4

Ingredients:

- 3 mahi mahi fillets (roughly 6–7 ounces each)
- ½ cup tapioca flour

- ⅓ cup almond flour
- 1 tablespoon onion powder
- 1 ½ teaspoons salt
- 2 eggs
- 3 tablespoons coconut oil
- 1 lime

Directions:

1. Cut the mahi mahi fillets into about 1.5″x1.5″ cubes using a kitchen knife. Place aside.

2. Tapioca flour, almond flour, onion powder, and salt should all be combined in a large basin or container.

3. The eggs should be whisked in their own basin or container.

4. Heat a sizable skillet on medium-high before adding the coconut oil.

5. Mahi bites should be added to the beaten eggs in batches before being added to the flour mixture. The fish should be evenly coated with the batter.

6. Put the fish in the heated coconut oil and fry it for one minute. Then, using kitchen tongs, turn the pieces over and cook them for an additional 45 to 1 minute. After that, flip the fish pieces on their unfried sides for about 30 seconds, or just long enough for all sides to become golden. To avoid overfilling the pan, you may need to work in batches.

7. Before serving, cut the lime in half and spritz with lime juice.

Nutritional Information: Calories 921; Fat 50g; Sodium 934mg; Carbs 88.9g; Fiber 44g; Sugar 3g; Protein 30g

Lemongrass Shrimp/Chicken Soup

Preparation time: 15 minutes
Cooking time: 20 minutes

Serves: 4

Ingredients:

- 6 cups stock, preferably organic chicken, beef, or vegetable
- 2 tsp lemongrass, frozen
- 3-4 lime leaves
- 3 to 4 cloves garlic, minced
- 1 slice of ginger around the size of the index finger
- 3 tbsp fish sauce or 4 tsp soy sauce (use wheat-free soy sauce for gluten-free diets)
- 1 tbsp lime juice, freshly squeezed
- 1 fresh red chili pepper or half a tsp of dried chili powder
- Vegetables (mushrooms, cauliflower, bok choy, broccoli), as you like
- 30 shrimp or 3 chicken breasts, cooked
- ½ can coconut milk
- 12 cups of fresh basil/cilantro

Directions:

1. The first four ingredients should be heated to a boil after being combined.
2. Add the remaining ingredients, minus the final three, and reduce the heat to somewhere between low and medium.
3. simmer for about 15 minutes.

4. Mix the meat thoroughly after adding a small amount of coconut milk.
5. Cook the food for an additional three to five minutes.
6. Before setting the bowls on the table, add a finishing touch by sprinkling chopped cilantro or basil over the top of each bowl's portion.

Nutritional Information: Calories 597; Fat 35.8g; Sodium 887mg; Carbs 12g; Fiber 2.8g; Sugar 4.8g; Protein 58g

Grilled Chicken Skewers

Preparation time: 10 minutes
Cooking time: 10 minutes
Serves: 4

Ingredients:

- 1 ¼ pounds skinless, boneless chicken breast halves
- ¾ cup Pace® Picante Sauce
- 1 tbsp vegetable oil
- 1 tbsp lime juice
- 1 garlic clove, minced or ¼ tsp garlic powder
- ½ tsp ground cumin

Directions:

1. Put two layers of plastic wrap on the chicken. Pluck the chicken and pound it with a rolling pin or a meat mallet to a thickness of 12 inch. Add salt and pepper to taste when preparing the chicken. Slice into 1-inch-long strips.
2. Combine the oil, cumin, lime juice, garlic powder, and picante sauce in a small bowl. Add the chicken and coat.
3. Thread the chicken onto the 8 skewers in an accordion fashion. Lightly oil the grill rack and preheat it to medium heat. Cook the chicken on the grill for 10 minutes, turning it over frequently, and basting with the Picante sauce mixture. Any remaining Picante sauce mixture must be thrown away.

Nutritional Information: Calories 215; Fat 7g; Sodium 395mg; Carbs 3.7g; Fiber 1.5g; Sugar 3g; Protein 32g

Asian Chicken and Rice Dish

Preparation time: 15 minutes
Cooking time: 35 minutes
 Serves: 6

Ingredients:

- 2–3 tbsp olive oil
- 1 onion, chopped
- 4 cloves garlic, chopped
- 1 pound chicken thighs, boneless and skinless, cut into bite-size pieces
- 1 whole red bell pepper or 1 cup tomatoes (drained, seeded, chopped)
- 1 cup uncooked long-grain rice (Jasmine recommended)
- 2 cups chicken broth
- 1 cup coconut milk, from canned (shake well before use)
- 2 tbsp regular soy sauce
- 2 tsp Asian fish sauce
- 1–2 tsp chili powder, depending on desired heat
- ¼ cup freshly chopped Thai basil
- Garnishes: lime wedges, roasted chopped peanuts

Directions:

1. In a sizable nonstick skillet, heat the oil over medium-high heat. In a skillet, cook the onion until it is soft. For one more minute, stir in the garlic. If more oil is required, add it. The chicken is added and stirred for 2–3 minutes, or until just barely browned.
2. In a sizing mixing bowl, combine the bell peppers or tomatoes, rice, broth, coconut milk, soy sauce, fish sauce, and chili powder. Bring to a boil, then immediately lower the heat to a simmer. Cook the rice covered on the stovetop for another 20 minutes, or until the rice is tender and the liquid has been absorbed.
3. Remove from the heat and leave covered for 10 minutes. Serve immediately with lime wedges and peanuts after gently tossing with Thai basil.

Nutritional Information: Calories 566; Fat 33.3g; Sodium 664mg; Carbs 31.5g; Fiber 2g; Sugar 3g; Protein 34.8g

Spicy Chicken Nuggets

Preparation time: 8 minutes
Cooking time: 20 minutes
Serves: 8

Ingredients:

- 1 cup all-purpose flour
- 4 tsp seasoned salt
- 1 tsp poultry seasoning
- 1 tsp ground mustard
- 1 tsp paprika
- ½ tsp pepper
- 2 pounds boneless and skinless chicken breasts

Directions:

1. In a large shallow dish, combine the first six ingredients. Chicken should be flattened to a thickness of 12 inch before being cut into 1-12 inch pieces. A few pieces of chicken at a time, place on platter, and mix with sauce.
2. Fry the chicken in a pan with the canola oil over medium-high heat until it forms a crust.
3. Dispense and savor!

Nutritional Information: Calories 260; Fat 10g; Sodium 634mg; Carbs 13g; Fiber 1g; Sugar 0.3g; Protein 27g

Dijon Salmon

Preparation time: 10 minutes
Cooking time: 15 minutes
Serves: 3

Ingredients:

- 5 tbsp low-fat plain Greek yogurt
- 2 tbsp Dijon mustard
- 2 tsp worth of chopped fresh dill

- 4 fresh garlic cloves, minced
- 4 tbsp fresh lemon juice, freshly squeezed
- ½chili powder, to taste
- 4 5-ounce salmon fillets

Directions:

1. Turn on the broiler and get it ready.
2. Combine the Greek yogurt, mustard, dill, garlic, lemon juice, and chili powder in a small bowl and stir to combine.
3. Arrange the salmon fillets on the broiler pan in a single layer and spray with Pam cooking spray. Broil the pan in the oven.

4. Place the salmon on a rack that is three inches away from the heat source of the broiler after coating it with the sauce.
5. Place the chicken for 5 to 6 minutes in the broiler.
6. Remove the salmon from the broiler and bake it in the oven at 425°F for an additional 6-7 minutes.
7. Take the dish out of the oven, and then start serving it.

Nutritional Information: Calories 267; Fat 8.3g; Sodium 257mg; Carbs 6.4g; Fiber 1.2g; Sugar 2.5g; Protein 40.5g

Enticing Grilled Tomatoes and Shrimp

Preparation time: 5 minutes
Cooking time: 5 minutes
Serves: 2

Ingredients:

- 2 cloves garlic, diced or minced, optional.
- 4 tbsp olive oil
- 1 tomato, chopped, medium-sized
- 1 tbsp vinegar, made from red wine
- 2 tbsp fresh basil, chopped
- the black pepper and the salt (to taste)

- 1 pound raw shrimp, peeled.

Directions:

1. In a blender, combine the garlic, olive oil, tomato, vinegar, basil, salt, and pepper. Blend until smooth. Blend until no lumps remain.
2. After putting the shrimp in a bowl, add the mixture on top of them.
3. Place the bowl in the coldest part of the refrigerator for a full hour.

4. Heat the grill to a medium temperature before igniting the charcoal.
5. Skewer the shrimp and cook them until they are fully cooked.
6. Spray the grill with Pam cooking spray, add the shrimp, and cook for two minutes on each side.
7. Indulge in this delectable main dish and the side dish of your choice, then enjoy the meal.

Nutritional Information: Calories 492; Fat 30.3g; Sodium 1979mg; Carbs 5.7g; Fiber 1.2g; Sugar 2.8g; Protein 47.6g

Balsamic Grilled Basa

Preparation time: 8 minutes
Cooking time: 10 minutes
Serves: 4
Ingredients:.
- 4 3.5-ounce basa fillets
- 1 tsp fresh rosemary, chopped
- the black pepper and the salt (to taste)
- ½ cup balsamic vinegar
- 1 tbsp extra-virgin olive oil
- 4 tbsp lemon juice, freshly squeezed
- 4 ½ cups baby spinach

Directions:.

1. Mix the vinegar, lemon juice, and olive oil in a bowl and whisk to combine.
2. After drizzling the salmon with the marinade, place it in the fridge for about 45 minutes so it can soak up the flavors.
3. Remove the fish from the fridge, then season it with the herbs and spices.

4. Lay the fillets out on the grill in a single layer and grill them for about 5 minutes on each side, or until the fish starts to flake.
6. Position the plate so it is resting on baby spinach.

Nutritional Information: Calories 232; Fat 13g; Sodium 99mg; Carbs 7.7g; Fiber 0.8g; Sugar 5.3g; Protein 19.5g

Balsamic Chicken Breast

Preparation time: 10 minutes plus 12 hours for marinating
Cooking time: 10 minutes
Serves: 5
Ingredients:
- 5 medium-sized chicken breast halves, skinless and boneless, without the skin, about 1 pound in total
- ¼ cup balsamic vinegar
- 2 fresh garlic cloves, crushed
- 14 tsp black pepper, ground
- 12 medium lemon, peeled and chopped into cubes
- 3 tsp Dijon mustard

Directions:
1. Combine all of the ingredients, excluding the chicken breasts, in a blender.
2. Pour the ingredients over the chicken, cover, and place in the refrigerator to marinate for at least 12 hours.

3 .Remove the chicken from the marinade and put it aside.

4. Place the chicken breasts on the grill and cook them for 5 minutes on each side over direct high heat.

5 .Place on a serving platter and eat with the vegetables or carbs of your choosing.

Nutritional Information: Calories 212; Fat 9g; Sodium 96mg; Carbs 14.8g; Fiber 2g; Sugar 4.9g; Protein 20g

Garlic Shrimp Etouffee

Preparation time: 15 minutes

Cooking time: 25 minutes

Serves: 4

Ingredients:

- 3 tbsp lard
- 1 small sweet onion diced
- 1 stalk celery diced
- ½ bell pepper diced (AIP: sub 1 more stalk celery or 1 small carrot)
- ¼ cup cassava flour
- 2 large cloves garlic pressed
- 1 tbsp Cajun seasoning or ½ tsp garlic powder, ½ tsp onion powder, ¼ tsp Italian seasoning, 1 tsp ginger powder, 1 tsp horseradish powder, and ¼ tsp Himalayan salt
- 1 tbsp dried parsley
- ½ tsp Himalayan salt
- 1 to 2 tsp Frank's Red Hot or lemon juice
- 1 pound medium shrimp peeled, deveined, tails removed and strained very well
- 3 cups bone broth, fish, chicken or pork
- 1 bay leaf
- lemon wedges

Directions:

1. SAUTÉ, please. Add the fat, onion, celery, and bell pepper when the dish starts to smell hot. Mix well.
2. Cook for 7 minutes or until browned and slightly caramelized, stirring occasionally.
3.
CANCEL, then vigorously stir in the cassava flour until the mixture comes together. Add salt, pepper, Cajun spice, garlic, and spicy sauce while stirring.

4. Please SAUTÉ. Once LESS is lit up, press ADJUST.
5. Pour in 1 cup of the bone broth while continually stirring to avoid lumps. Once the mixture is smooth, add the bay leaf and gradually whisk in the remaining 2 cups of broth.
6. Simmer while stirring and scraping the bottom every few minutes to avoid sticking. Cook in this manner for 10 to 15 minutes, or until the sauce has thickened and been reduced to 2/3.
7. Add shrimp and stir. Cook for two minutes while stirring constantly. Click CANCEL.
8. Shrimp will continue to cook slightly in the hot gravy, so it is best to turn off the heat below just before they appear to be finished.)
9. With lemon wedges and a splash of hot sauce, serve in bowls.

 Nutritional Information: Calories 253; Fat 10.8g; Sodium 1290mg; Carbs 14.6g; Fiber 1.6g; Sugar 5.4g; Protein 25g

Chicken Meatloaf

Preparation time: 15 minutes
Cooking time: 45 minutes
Serves: 8
Ingredients:
- 5 ½ pounds lean ground chicken

117

- 1 medium onion
- 1 green pepper
- 12 cups zucchini
- 12 cups broccoli
- 2 stalks celery
- 1 ounce chopped up mushrooms
- 1 tsp thyme
- ¼ cup fresh basil
- ¼ cup fresh parsley
- salt and pepper, to taste
- 4 egg whites.
- 2 cups rolled organic oats in the organic form
- 1 bulb garlic, minced

Directions:

1. Spray a skillet with Pam cooking spray before adding the onions, peppers, zucchini, broccoli, celery, and mushrooms. Cook the vegetables for a few minutes over medium heat.

2. Add garlic. 1 to 2 minutes prior to the vegetables being finished cooking, turn off the heat, and then let the vegetables cool for about 5 minutes.

3. Add the cooked veggies and the other ingredients to a large dish and stir everything together.

4. Before putting the batter in the oven, place it in loaf pans or any other baking dish that has been greased with Pam.

5. Cook in an oven that has been preheated to 425°F for a total of 40 minutes.

6. After taking the meatloaf out of the oven, allow it to cool for 45 minutes before serving.

7. Eat the chicken after cutting it into 8 equal pieces.

Nutritional Information: Calories 600; Fat 27.8g; Sodium 395mg; Carbs 26g; Fiber 6g; Sugar 8g; Protein 64g

Lemony Shrimp with Cocktail Sauce

Preparation time: 10 minutes
Cooking time: 5 minutes
Serves: 8

Ingredients:

- 2 cups water
- 1 tbsp sea salt
- 2 pounds large or jumbo shrimp deveined, fresh or frozen
- 2 lemons
- Ice bath

Cocktail sauce:

- ¾ cup sugar-free ketchup
- 1 ½ tbsp horseradish
- 1 tbsp apple cider vinegar
- 1 tsp lemon juice
- 1 tsp coconut aminos
- ½ tsp hot sauce

Directions:

1. Prepare the coffee sauce by whisking all of the ingredients together. While you cook the shrimp, refrigerate.
2. Fill the Instant Pot with water and sea salt.
3. Cut the lemons in half, squeeze the juice into the pot, and then add the lemon halves.

4. Add the shrimp and combine.
5. Secure the Instant Pot and switch the steam release knob to Sealing.
6. Cook for 30 seconds on High if the shrimp has defrosted. While the shrimp is cooking, prepare an ice bath. Quick release pressure.
7. Cook frozen shrimp for one minute on high. During the cooking of the shrimp, prepare an ice bath. Quick release pressure.

8. Transfer the shrimp to the ice bath with a slotted spoon so they can stop cooking.

Peel the shrimp. 9 To have something to grip onto while eating, I like to leave the tail on.

10. Offer with a cocktail auce.

Nutritional Information: Calories 126; Fat 0.7g; Sodium 1247mg; Carbs 8g; Fiber 0.6g; Sugar 5.4g; Protein 23g

Oregano Chicken Tacos Salad

Preparation time: 10 minutes
Cooking time: 15 to 20 minutes
Serves: 3
Ingredients:
- ⅔ pound chicken or turkey ground meat
- 1 yellow onion, cut into 12 large slices
- dried red pepper, chopped
- 1 level tsp dried oregano
- 2 tsp chili pepper
- ½ tsp black pepper
- 1 packet stevia
- 1 small can chopped tomatoes, drained
- Salt to taste
- 6 romaine lettuce leaves

Directions:

1. Use Pam cooking spray to coat a medium-sized saucepan and heat it over a flame between medium and high.
2. Add the onions and peppers when the oil has entirely been absorbed, and continue to cook the combination until the onions are transparent.
3. Combine the other ingredients well before serving, excluding the canned tomatoes and the lettuce.

4. Combine the ingredients in a saucepan and bring the mixture to a boil. Once the chicken or turkey has been ground, continue with this step.

5. Turn off the heat and pour off any liquid that has accumulated in the pan.

6. Re-heat it on the burner, this time with the heat set to a temperature that lies halfway between medium and low, and then stir in the canned tomatoes.

7. After you've finished cooking, continue for an additional 5 minutes. Serve it to the visitors after taking it off the heat.

8. There are two ways to prepare this dish: either slice the romaine lettuce and serve it as a salad with the chicken mixture on top, or use the individual romaine leaves as taco shells and fill each one with the chicken mixture.

Nutritional Information: Calories 343; Fat 12g; Sodium 1170mg; Carbs 32g; Fiber 7g; Sugar 11.7g; Protein 32g

Mahi Mahi Taco

Preparation time: 4 minutes
Cooking time: 15 minutes
Serves: 2
Ingredients:
- 4 cups shredded cabbage
- 2 filets mahi mahi, about 4 ounces each
- 2 cups riced cauliflower
- 1 tbsp taco seasoning
- ½ cup mango salsa
- ½ tablespoon plus 1 teaspoon avocado oil
- 1 tablespoon lime juice
- ¼ cup cilantro, roughly chopped
- 2 tablespoons spicy chipotle mayo
- ½ large avocado

- ½ cup red onion, thinly sliced
- ½ cup apple cider vinegar
- water
- 1 teaspoon salt
- optional toppings: jalapeños, cilantro, lime wedges

Directions:

1. Make the indicated choices. Add salt, water, apple cider vinegar, and other ingredients to a jar. Set aside after vigorously shaking.
2. Prepare the cauliflower dish. Heat a sizable skillet on low heat and add one tsp of oil. For 4-5 minutes, add the mince. Combine cilantro and lime juice, then set aside.
3. Spread taco seasoning evenly over the fish. Heat the same pan to medium and add the remaining oil. Incorporate the fish, cook for 3 minutes, flip, and cook for an additional 2–3 minutes, depending on thickness.

4. Put together the bowls. Separate the cabbage, cauliflower rice, salsa, avocado, and chipotle mayo into two bowls. Top each bowl with a fish filet and your favorite garnishes; I used jalapenos, lime wedges, and cilantro. Enjoy!

Nutritional Information: Calories 685; Fat 76g; Sodium 2113mg; Carbs 36g; Fiber 11.6g; Sugar 14.4g; Protein 76g

Snack and Appetizer Recipes

Garlic Salsa

Preparation time: 10 minutes
Cooking time: 2 ½ hours to 3 hours
Serves: 25

Ingredients:

- 10 plum tomatoes
- 2 garlic cloves
- 1 small onion, cut into wedges
- 1–2 jalapeño peppers
- ½ cup chopped fresh cilantro
- ½ tsp sea salt, optional

Directions:

1. Take off the tomatoes' cores. Make a tiny slit in each tomato. A garlic clove should be placed in each slice.
2. Put all of the tomatoes and onions in a 3-quart slow cooker.
3. Cut the jalapenos' stems off. (If you want a milder version, remove the seeds.) The jalapenos should be put in a slow cooker.

4. Covered, cook on high for 2 to 3 hours, or until the vegetables are soft. Some might start to turn brown. Give the lid some time to cool for at least two hours. The tomato mixture, cilantro, and salt, if desired, should all be combined in a blender. Blend until combined while covered.

Nutritional Information: Calories 19; Fat 0g; Sodium 50mg; Carbs 4.9g; Fiber 0.3g; Sugar 4.4g; Protein 0.2g

Curried Almonds with Turmeric

Preparation time: 5 minutes

Cooking time: 3½–4½ hours
 Serves: 64

Ingredients:

- 2 tbsp coconut oil
- 1 tbsp curry powder
- ½ tsp sea salt
- ⅛ tsp turmeric
- ⅛ tsp paprika
- ⅛ tsp onion powder
- ⅛ tsp garlic powder
- ⅛ tsp sugar
- 1 pound blanched almonds

Directions:

1. In a mixing bowl, combine the spices and coconut oil.
2. Fill the slow cooker with the liquid, then add the almonds. To coat, thoroughly combine.
3. Cover. 2 to 3 hours on low heat. Turn up the volume all the way. After revealing the cooker, cook for 1 to 1 1/2 hours.
4. Serve warm or at room temperature.

Nutritional Information: Calories 45; Fat 4g; Sodium 18mg; Carbs 1.6g; Fiber 1g; Sugar 0.3g; Protein 1.5g

Mexican Meat Dip

Preparation time: 15 to 20 minutes
Cooking time: 2 to 3 hours
Serves: 15

Ingredients:

- 1 pound low-fat ground beef or turkey
- 1 8-ounce package low-fat Mexican cheese, grated
- 1 16-ounce jar mild, thick, and chunky Picante salsa, or thick and chunky salsa

- 1 6-ounce can vegetarian refried beans

Directions:

1. In a nonstick skillet, brown the meat.
2. In your crock, combine the meat and the other ingredients.
3. Cook for 3 hours on low, or until all ingredients are thoroughly cooked and melted.
4. Top with a jalapeo.

Nutritional Information: Calories 162; Fat 8g; Sodium 638mg; Carbs 10g; Fiber 0.6g; Sugar 0.2g; Protein 12.6g

Awesome Seven-Layer Dip

Preparation time: 20 minutes
Cooking time: 2 hours
Serves: 10 to 15

Ingredients:

- 1 pound lean ground turkey
- 2½ tsp chili powder, divided
- ½ tsp kosher salt
- ⅛ tsp pepper
- 1 15-ounce can fat-free refried beans
- 1 4-ounce can diced green chilies
- 1 cup non-fat Greek yogurt
- 1 cup salsa
- 1 cup shredded Mexican blend cheese
- 1 2-ounce can sliced black olives
- 2 green onions, sliced

Directions:

1. In a pan, brown the ground turkey with a tsp of chili powder, salt, and pepper.
2. In the meantime, apply nonstick cooking spray to the crock.
3. Layer the refried beans in a layer on the bottom of the crock after mixing them with 1 tsp of chili powder.

4. After that, layer the green chilies in dice on top.

5. Distribute the ground turkey equally over the green chilies.

6.Combine the Greek yogurt and the remaining 1/2 tsp chili powder in a mixing bowl.Pour the mixture over the ground turkey in the crock.

7. Last but not least, add the salsa on top.

8. Place the black olives on top, then put the cheese on top of that.

9. Cook for two hours on low. Before serving, top with the green onions.

Nutritional Information: Calories 139; Fat 6.6g; Sodium 666mg; Carbs 10g; Fiber 4.6g; Sugar 2.2g; Protein 12g

Herbed Pizza Dip

Preparation time: 15 minutes
Cooking time: 5 to 6 hours
Serves: 14
Ingredients:
- 1 pound bulk gluten-free turkey sausage
- ⅔ cup chopped onion
- 4 cloves garlic, minced
- 2 15-ounce cans low-sodium tomato sauce
- 1 14.5-ounce can diced tomatoes
- 1 6-ounce can low-sodium tomato paste
- 1 tbsp dried oregano
- 1 tbsp dried basil
- ¾ tsp crushed red pepper
- 1½ tsp turbinado sugar
- ½ cup sliced black olives

Directions:

1. In a big skillet, cook the onion, garlic, and turkey sausage. Take the grease off.

2. Except for the olives, combine all of the remaining ingredients in the crock.

3.Cook, covered, on low for 5 to 6 hours. Just prior to serving, stir in the olives.

4. To make it more nutritious, serve it with a rainbow of bell pepper slices for dipping. Garnish options include minced parsley or microgreens.

Nutritional Information: Calories 149; Fat 9g; Sodium 381mg; Carbs 8.5g; Fiber 2g; Sugar 5g; Protein 8.7g

Veggie and Cheese Dip

Preparation time: 10 minutes
Cooking time: 3 to 4 hours
 Serves: 3
Ingredients:
- 1 10-ounce bag fresh baby spinach, roughly chopped
- 1 13.75-ounce can quartered artichoke hearts, drained and chopped
- 1 8-ounce brick reduced-fat cream cheese
- 1 cup non-fat plain Greek yogurt
- 1 cup shredded mozzarella cheese
- ½ cup grated Parmesan cheese
- ½ cup chopped onion
- ¼ cup chopped green onion

Directions:

1. Spray nonstick cooking spray on your crock.
2. All the ingredients should be combined and thoroughly stirred in a big crock.
3. for three to four hours on low, covered, or until the cheese has completely melted and the dip is thoroughly heated.

4. Serve with fresh carrot sticks, gluten-free pita bread, or brown rice crackers. Add sliced red bell pepper as a garnish.

Nutritional Information: Calories 164; Fat 6.6g; Sodium 388mg; Carbs 13g; Fiber 5.6g; Sugar 4g; Protein 15g

Garlic Chicken Lettuce Wraps

Preparation time: 15 minutes
Cooking time: 2 to 3 hours
Serves: 12
Ingredients:

- 2 pounds ground chicken, browned
- 4 cloves garlic, minced
- ½ cup minced sweet yellow onion
- 4 tbsp gluten-free soy sauce or Bragg's liquid aminos
- 1 tbsp natural crunchy peanut butter
- 1 tsp rice wine vinegar
- 1 tsp sesame oil
- ¼ tsp kosher salt
- ¼ tsp red pepper flakes
- ¼ tsp black pepper
- 1 8-ounce can sliced water chestnuts, drained, rinsed, chopped
- 3 green onions, sliced
- 12 good-sized pieces of iceberg lettuce, rinsed and patted dry

Directions:

1. Combine the ground chicken, peanut butter, vinegar, sesame oil, liquid aminos, garlic, yellow onion, salt, red pepper flakes, and black pepper in the cooker.
2. Cook, covered, on low for two to three hours.
3. Add the water chestnuts and green onions. Cook covered for another 10 to 15 minutes.

4. Each iceberg lettuce leaf should receive a generous amount.
5. Garnish with diced green onion and red bell pepper when serving.

Nutritional Information: Calories 170; Fat 7.6g; Sodium 280mg; Carbs 13g; Fiber 2.6g; Sugar 1.8g; Protein 15g

Savory Balsamic Sausage Bites

Preparation time: 15 minutes
Cooking time: 4 to 6 hours
Serves: 18 to 20
Ingredients:
- 1 medium sweet yellow onion, sliced
- 2 sweet apples, peeled, cored, sliced
- 2 pounds chicken apple sausage links, sliced into ½" rounds
- 4 tbsp spicy brown mustard
- 4 tbsp balsamic vinegar
- ⅓ cup honey

Directions:
1. Apply nonstick cooking spray to your crock.
2. Place the onions, apples, and sausages in a layer on the bottom of the crock.
3. In a mixing bowl, combine the honey, balsamic vinegar, and mustard. Pour this over the food in the slow cooker.

4 . Cook covered on low for 4-6 hours. To serve, toothpicks are employed.

Nutritional Information: Calories 67; Fat 0.4g; Sodium 38mg; Carbs 16.7g; Fiber 1.6g; Sugar 14.6g; Protein 0.4g

Hoisin Button Mushrooms

Preparation time: 10 minutes
Cooking time: 5 to 6 hours
Serves: 10

Ingredients:

- 24 ounces whole button mushrooms, trimmed
- 1 small sweet onion, halved, sliced
- ¼ cup water
- 3 cloves garlic, minced
- 2 tbsp gluten-free soy sauce or Bragg's liquid aminos
- 1 tbsp smooth natural peanut butter
- 1 tsp rice wine vinegar
- 1 tsp sesame oil
- ¼ tsp crushed red pepper

Directions:

1. Spray nonstick cooking spray on the crock.
2. Add the mushrooms and onions to the crock.
3. In a sizing mixing bowl, combine the water, garlic, soy sauce, peanut butter, rice wine vinegar, sesame oil, and crushed red pepper. Pouring this mixture over the mushrooms and onions is necessary.

4. Covered, cook on low for 5 to 6 hours.
5. Before removing the mushrooms with a slotted spoon for serving, gently fold them into the sauce. The mushrooms are served on toothpicks.
6. Garnish with sliced green onion and sesame seeds.

Nutritional Information: Calories 228; Fat 1.8g; Sodium 124mg; Carbs 54.9g; Fiber 8.3g; Sugar 3.4g; Protein 7.6g

Boiled Unshelled Peanuts

Preparation time: 5 minutes
Cooking time: 7 to 8 hours
Serves: 32

Ingredients:
- 2 pounds raw peanuts in the shell
- 7 tbsp salt water to cover peanuts

Directions:

1. Unshelled peanuts should be thoroughly cleaned in cold water.
2. In your slow cooker crock, soak the peanuts over night in water with 7 tsp of salt.
3. Early in the morning, lower the heat to low and cook the peanuts for 7 to 10 hours, or until they are mushy. Boiling peanuts should have soft, pliable shells rather than crispy, rigid ones.

4. Before serving, drain the peanuts and let them cool for ten minutes. Eat the peanuts after removing their shells.
5. Any leftover cooked peanuts should be refrigerated or frozen. Reheat the meal before serving.

Nutritional Information: Calories 160; Fat 13.8g; Sodium 3mg; Carbs 4.7g; Fiber 2.4g; Sugar 1g; Protein 7g

Gingered Nuts Mix

Preparation time: 15 minutes
Cooking time: 2 hours
Serves: 22

Ingredients:
- 1 cup unsalted cashews
- 1 cup unsalted almonds
- 1 cup unsalted pecans
- 1 cup unsalted, shelled pistachios

- ½ cup maple syrup
- ⅓ cup melted coconut oil
- 1 tsp ground ginger
- ½ tsp sea salt
- ½ tsp cinnamon
- ¼ tsp ground cloves
- ¼ tsp cayenne pepper

Directions:

1. Spray nonstick cooking spray on the crock.
2. Add the nuts to the crock and stir in the other ingredients, making sure they are all evenly distributed.
3. Before covering the crock, slide a piece of paper towel or a thin dishtowel underneath the lid. Cook on low heat for an hour, then stir in the nuts. After two hours, stir them once more, then spread them out on a cookie sheet covered with parchment paper. Allow for cooling for an hour.

4. You can either serve the nuts right away or store any leftovers for up to three weeks in an airtight jar.

Nutritional Information: Calories 194; Fat 16.4g; Sodium 55mg; Carbs 10.4g; Fiber 2g; Sugar 5.6g; Protein 4g

Almond, Cranberry, and Coconut

Preparation time: 10 minutes
Cooking time: 2 to 3 hours
Serves: 12
Ingredients:

- 5 cups gluten-free Cheerios
- 3 cups gluten-free Honey Nut Cheerios
- 1 cup gluten-free oats
- 1 cup dried cranberries

- 2 cups unsweetened shredded coconut
- 2 cups raw almonds, chopped
- ¼ cup melted coconut oil
- ¼ cup honey
- ½ tsp cinnamon
- ½ tsp salt
- 1 tsp vanilla

Directions:

1. Spray nonstick cooking spray on the crock.
2. Cheerios, Honey Nut Cheerios, gluten-free oats, cranberries, coconut, and almonds should be used to fill the middle of the crock.
3 .In a mixing bowl, combine the coconut oil, honey, cinnamon, salt, and vanilla. With a rubber spatula, gently stir the cereal in the crock after adding the mixture to make sure it is all coated.

4. With a paper towel under the lid, cover the pot and cook it for two to three hours on low. Stir the mixture about every 45 minutes to prevent burning.
5. After the mixture has finished cooking, pour it onto a baking sheet that has been lined with parchment paper and leave it there to cool for an hour. Serve right away or store for up to 3 weeks at room temperature in an airtight jar.

Nutritional Information: Calories 252; Fat 10g; Sodium 230mg; Carbs 42.5g; Fiber 3.5g; Sugar 16g; Protein 3.7g

Lemony Artichokes

Preparation time: 20 minutes
Cooking time: 2 to 10 hours
Serves: 4
Ingredients:
- 4 artichokes

- 1 tsp salt
- 2 tbsp lemon juice

Directions:

1. Artichokes should be washed and trimmed, with the tops being trimmed by 3/4 to 1 inch and the stems being cut flush with the bottoms. Stand straight inside the slow cooker.

2. Pour over the artichokes the salt and lemon juice you've combined in a bowl.

3.Add enough water to the artichokes to cover 34% of them.

4. Cover. 2-4 hours on high or 8–10 hours on low.

5. Put a dollop of melted butter on top before serving.

Nutritional Information: Calories 62; Fat 0.2g; Sodium 702mg; Carbs 14g; Fiber 7g; Sugar 1.5g; Protein 4g

Mayo Deviled Eggs with Veggies

Preparation time: 8 minutes
Cooking time: None
Serves: 8

Ingredients:

- 8 hard-boiled eggs, peeled
- 4 tsp mayonnaise
- 14 cups cooked spinach
- 2 ounces chopped artichokes
- ½ tsp Dijon mustard
- ¼ cup grated Parmesan cheese
- ½ tsp powdered garlic
- 1 tsp salt
- ½ tsp black pepper

Directions:

1. Cut hard-boiled eggs in half lengthwise before consuming.in a bowl, scoop the egg yolks.

2 .Mayonnaise, spinach, artichokes, mustard, garlic powder, Parmesan cheese, salt, and pepper should all be combined in a medium mixing bowl. Mash the mixture with a fork until a paste forms.

3 .The mixture can be spooned or piped into the egg white cavities.

4. Before serving, top with paprika, sumac, Parmesan cheese, or chopped herbs. (selected by you)

Nutritional Information: Calories 228; Fat 12g; Sodium 699mg; Carbs 14.4g; Fiber 8g; Sugar 2g; Protein 19.7g

Garlic Flaxseed Crackers

Preparation time: 5 minutes
Cooking time: 30 minutes
Serves: 1

Ingredients:
- 1 cup ground flaxseed
- 1 tsp powdered garlic
- 1 tsp powdered onion
- 1 tsp cayenne pepper
- ½ cup water

Directions:
1. Fill an appropriate mixing bowl with all of the ingredients.
2. Add the water and stir until a dough forms.
3. Give the dough 10 minutes to firm up.

4. Spread the dough out on a baking sheet covered with parchment paper. With the aid of a second piece of parchment paper, roll the dough into a narrow rectangle.
5. Using a sharp knife, cut into squares.

6. Place the squares on a baking sheet that has been lined with parchment paper.
7. Bake for 30 minutes at 400°F, rotating the pan halfway through to ensure crispness on both sides.

Nutritional Information: Calories 921; Fat 71g; Sodium 57mg; Carbs 53.7g; Fiber 47g; Sugar 3g; Protein 31.7g

Dijon Stuffed Eggs

Preparation time: 10 minutes
Cooking time: 10 minutes
Serves: 2
Ingredients:
- Approximately 8-10 hard-boiled eggs
- 5 spears of asparagus
- 3 tsp mayonnaise
- ½ tsp Dijon mustard
- 2 finely chopped spring onions
- 1 tsp capers, chopped
- ½ tsp salt
- ½ tsp black pepper
- 1 tbsp chopped chives for garnish

Directions:
1. Trim the asparagus stalks' crowns and remove the rough bottom end. The tips should be set aside for decorating.
2. The remaining stalks are added after halfway filling the pot with water. Until soft, simmer for 10 minutes with a lid on after bringing it to a boil.
3. Asparagus stalks should be drained and carefully sliced.

4. Hard-boiled eggs: Halve them after removing the yolks and setting the whites aside. In a bowl, mix together the egg yolks, asparagus spears, mayonnaise, spring onions, capers, and mustard.

5. To taste, add salt and pepper to the food.
6. Pour the mixture halfway into a piping bag and then pipe it into the hard-boiled eggs. Or you may spoon the mixture in.
7. Place the asparagus tip, cut into quarters, atop the eggs.
8. Sprinkle the chopped chives on top of the eggs.
9. Enjoy and consume!

Nutritional Information: Calories 375; Fat 25g; Sodium 914mg; Carbs 5.7g; Fiber 0.9g; Sugar 3.4g; Protein 29g

Creamy Seafood Dip

Preparation time: 5 to 10 minutes
Cooking time: 3 hours
Serves: 3

Ingredients:

- 1 10-ounce package fat-free cream cheese
- 1 8-ounce package imitation crab strands
- 2 tbsp onion, finely chopped
- 4–5 drops hot sauce
- ¼ cup walnuts, finely chopped
- 1 tsp paprika

Directions:

1. Blend each ingredient in the blender, with the exception of the nuts and paprika, until well combined.
2. In a slow cooker, arrange. Add some nuts and paprika.
3. Cook on low for three hours.

4. Add paprika, cayenne pepper, and parsley or cilantro as garnishes.

Nutritional Information: Calories 55; Fat 3.7g; Sodium 149mg; Carbs 1.3g; Fiber 0.1g; Sugar 0.8g; Protein 4g

Fantastic Chex Mix

Preparation time: 8 minutes
Cooking time: 1 hour
Serves: 12

Ingredients:

- 3 cups gluten-free Rice Chex
- 3 cups gluten-free Corn Chex
- 3 cups gluten-free Cheerios
- 1 cup unsalted peanuts
- ⅓ cup coconut oil, melted
- 4 tsp gluten-free Worcestershire sauce
- 1 tsp sea salt
- 1 tsp garlic powder
- 1 tsp onion powder

Directions:

1. Spray nonstick cooking spray on the crock.
2. Put Cheerios, Rice Chex, Corn Chex, and peanuts in the crock.
3. In a small bowl, combine the Worcestershire sauce, sea salt, garlic powder, and onion powder with the coconut oil. This should be poured over the cereal in the crock and gently stirred with a rubber spatula until coated.

4. Cook on low for three hours with a lid made of paper towels or a thin dishcloth, stirring once after the first hour, twice after the second hour, and once after the third.
5. Spread the mixture out on parchment paper-lined baking sheets, then let them cool for an hour.
6. Use an airtight container for serving or storing.

Nutritional Information: Calories 398; Fat 20.3g; Sodium 270mg; Carbs 54.7g; Fiber 10.5g; Sugar 1.5g; Protein 11.5g

Unique Apple Butter

Preparation time: 20 minutes
Cooking time: 12 to 14 hours
Serves: 24

Ingredients:
- 4 pounds apples
- 2 tsp cinnamon
- ½ tsp ground cloves

Directions:
1. It is necessary to peel, core, and slice apples. Place all the ingredients in the slow cooker.
2. Over it, place a cover. on high for two to three hours. Turn down the heat to a low level and cook for eight hours. Apples should be half-cooked and have a deep brown hue.
3. Stir in the spices completely. Cook for two to three hours on high with the lid off. Stir the ingredients well until it is smooth.
4. Pour the mixture into freezer-safe containers and freeze them, or put the mixture in sterilized jars and seal them.

Nutritional Information: Calories 38; Fat 0.1g; Sodium 1mg; Carbs 10.2g; Fiber 2g; Sugar 7.6g; Protein 0.2g

Meatballs Enticing Turkey-Quinoa

Preparation time: 30 minutes
Cooking time: 6 hours
Serves: 8

Ingredients:
- 2 pounds lean ground turkey
- ⅔ cup cooked quinoa
- 6 cloves garlic, minced, divided
- 1 egg lightly beaten
- 2 tbsp grated Parmesan

- 3 tbsp Italian seasoning, divided
- 3 tsp onion powder, divided
- 1¾ tsp kosher salt
- 1 tsp pepper, divided
- 4 tbsp olive oil
- 2 28-ounce cans low-sodium crushed tomatoes
- 1 6-ounce can low-sodium tomato paste
- ¼ cup balsamic vinegar

Directions:

1. In a mixing dish, combine the ground turkey, quinoa, egg, Parmesan cheese, 1 tbsp Italian seasoning, 1 tsp onion powder, 34 tsp kosher salt, and 12 tsp pepper. Make meatballs measuring 12" out of the mixture.
2. Lightly brown each meatball on both sides in a large pan over medium-high heat, using 2 tbsp of olive oil. Take them out of the picture.
3. In a large mixing bowl, combine the tomato paste, crushed tomatoes, remaining 3 minced garlic cloves, 2 tbsp Italian seasoning, 2 tsp onion powder, 1 tsp kosher salt, 12 tsp pepper, 2 tbsp olive oil, and 1/4 cup balsamic vinegar.

4. Place all of the little meatballs on top of half of the tomato sauce mixture in the crock. Add the last bit of tomato sauce on top to complete the dish.
5. Covered, cook on low for 6 hours.
6. Garnish with chopped fresh basil or green onion slices and serve with fascinating ornamental toothpicks. 3 minuscule meatballs

Nutritional Information: Calories 371; Fat 20g; Sodium 1042mg; Carbs 19g; Fiber 3g; Sugar 10.5g; Protein 28g

Conclusion

The whole body reset is a weight loss program that encourages excellent health, a flat stomach, and a physique that people will appreciate well beyond middle age. It explains why traditional diet and exercise advice becomes ineffective as people age, and how minor dietary changes can prevent and even reverse age-related weight gain and muscle loss.The Whole Body Reset does not use calorie restriction, meal windows, stages of dieting, or any other popular techniques. The six fundamental secrets and various recipes in the book are easy to use and were created with regular people in mind.

Protein timing, or eating enough protein throughout the day, is one way to stop weight gain in middle age.This approach may help seniors alter not just their bodies but also their lifestyles when paired with a wealth of vitamins and minerals, fiber, and healthy fats.

This diet does not include calorie tracking or dietary restriction, is neither low in carbohydrates nor fat, and does not exclude any food categories. However, if you know how to incorporate it into your everyday life, it might stop and even reverse age-related muscle loss and weight gain. It might even improve your overall physical and mental health and make you less likely to get a number of long-term diseases that come with getting older.

Printed in Great Britain
by Amazon